Snapshots of Planet Earth

An Anthology of International Poetry

Edited by
Paul Richardson
Ken Watson
and Margaret Gill

Melbourne

OXFORD UNIVERSITY PRESS

OXFORD UNIVERSITY PRESS AUSTRALIA

Oxford   New York
Athens   Auckland   Bangkok   Bogota   Bombay
Buenos Aires   Calcutta   Cape Town   Dar es Salaam
Delhi   Florence   Hong Kong   Istanbul   Karachi
Kuala Lumpur   Madras   Madrid   Melbourne
Mexico City   Nairobi   Paris   Port Moresby
Singapore   Taipei   Tokyo   Toronto   Warsaw

and associated companies in
Berlin   Ibadan

OXFORD is a trade mark of Oxford University Press

O W L S
OXFORD DICTIONARY WORD
AND LANGUAGE SERVICE
Do you have a query about words, their
origin, meaning, use, spelling, pronun-
ciation, or any other aspect of interna-
tional English? Then write to OWLS
at the Australian National Dictionary
Centre, Australian National University,
Canberra, ACT 0200. All queries will
be answered using the full resources of
The Australian National Dictionary and
The Oxford English Dictionary.

National Library of Australia
Cataloguing-in-Publication data:

Snapshots of planet earth: an anthology of
international poetry.

Includes index.
ISBN 0 19 554182 0.

1. Poetry—Collections. I. Richardson, Paul (Paul W.).
II. Watson, Ken (Ken D.). III. Gill, Margaret, 1934– .

808.81

Edited by Frith Luton
Illustrated by Anna Wilson
Text designed by Lynn Twelftree
Cover designed by Caroline Laird
Cover illustration by Dimitrios Prokopis
Cover photographs from Coo-ee Picture Library,
Wendy Anderson, Caroline Laird and Ann Mudie
Typeset by Bookset, Type & Image
Printed by Kyodo Printing Co., Singapore
Published by Oxford University Press,
253 Normanby Road, South Melbourne, Australia

Contents

**An Introduction to Reading and
Teaching Poetry**   **1**

Words   **5**

Snapshots   *Gerda Mayer*   5
Words   *Catherine Fisher*   6
Consumer Poems   *Lawrence Sail*   6
The Television Poem   *Pete Morgan*   7
Pencil   *Robert Zend*   8
Thunderstorms   *W. H. Davis*   9
Living Language   *Jane Donald*   9
Notes   10
Activities   10

Action Shots   **12**

Snap Shot   *Philip Hodgins*   12
Drop Kick   *Philip Hodgins*   12
Place Kick   *Philip Hodgins*   13
Junior Coaching   *William Scammell* 14
The Surf-Rider   *Zulfikar Ghose*   15
The Surfer   *Judith Wright*   16
First Fight   *Vernon Scannell*   16
Notes   21
Activities   22

Multiple Exposures   **23**

Thirteen Ways of Looking at a
   Blackbird   *Wallace Stevens*   23
Thirteen Ways of Looking at a
   Blackboard   *Peter Redgrove*   25
Fourteen Ways of Touching the
   Peter   *George MacBeth*   27
The Red Wheelbarrow
   William Carlos Williams   29
The Poem William Carlos Williams

Never Wrote, but Might Have,
Had He lived on Mangoes
for a Year   *R. Palmateer*   29
Notes   30
Activities   30

Portraits   **31**

Car Salesman   *Colin Thiele*   31
from The Canterbury Tales
   Geoffrey Chaucer   32
from The Cantbeworried Tales
   The Advertising Agent
   The Real Estate Agent
   David Swain   32
Perfect Beggar   *David Gill*   34
The Angry Man   *Phyllis McGinley*   34
Simply Being Jim   *Ian Saw*   35
Warning   *Jenny Joseph*   36
'Ghost Wanted; Young, Willing'
   Bruce Dawe   37
Notes   38
Activities   38

Landscapes and Still Life   **41**

The Winter Pond   *Ai' Ch'ing*   41
Winter Afternoon
   Robert Adamson   42
Into the Landscape   *J. S. Harry*   42
The Song of the Whale   *Kit Wright* 43
Breakers   *Edward Lowbury*   44
Pine Tree   *Geoff Page*   44
Ash Wednesday   *Peter Macfarlane* 45
The Meaning   *Philip Hodgins*   46
Notes   48
Activities   48

Love and Other Catastrophes　49

Love　*Vernon Scannell*　49
I will give my love an apple　*Anon.*　50
Prize-Giving　*Gwen Harwood*　50
The Pop Star's Song
　Vernon Scannell　52
Scaffolding　*Seamus Heaney*　53
It's Raining in Love
　Richard Brautigan　53
Symptoms　*Sophie Hannah*　54
Stop All the Clocks　*W. H. Auden*　55
Love's Coming
　John Shaw Neilson　56
A Day Too Late　*Sophie Hannah*　56
Passengers to the City
　Katherine Gallagher　57
Suburban Lovers　*Bruce Dawe*　58
Dinner at My Sister's　*Bruce Dawe*　58
Unholy Marriage
　David Holbrook　59
The passionate Sheepheard to his
　love　*Christopher Marlowe*　60
The Nimphs reply to the Sheepheard
　Sir Walter Raleigh　61
Come Live With Me and be My Girl
　Leo Aylen　62
Notes　63
Activities　66

School and Other Disasters　67

Around the High School
　John Laue　67
The Play Way　*Seamus Heaney*　68
Novel Lesson　*Jeff Guess*　68
What's in a Locker?
　Fran Haraway　69
To Let Her Think Shadows
　B. A. Breen　70
The Spelling Prize
　Gwen Harwood　71
Examiner　*F. R. Scott*　73
The Examination
　Roger McGough　74

Whatever's the matter with Melanie?
　Barrie Wade　75
The Green Rambler
　Dennis DePauw　76
Mid-term Break　*Seamus Heaney*　77
Notes　78
Activities　79

Playing with Language　80

Not Enough Dough? Tough!
　William Random　80
Homophones　*George E. Coon*　82
Typo　*Russell Hoban*　83
The Anguish of the Machine
　Peter Murphy　84
Orgy　*Edwin Morgan*　85
The Hitch-hiker's Curse on Being
　Passed by　*John Birtwhistle*　86
To The Station　*J. R. Boothroyd*　87
Notes　89
Activities　89

Double Exposure　90

from The Emigrants
　Edward Brathwaite　90
Catching Crabs　*David Dabydeen*　92
They Come for the Islands (1493)
　Pablo Neruda　93
Migrant Woman on a Melbourne
　Tram　*Jennifer Strauss*　94
Immigrants at Central Station, 1951
　Peter Skrzynecki　95
Notes　96
Activities　96

Indigenous Images　97

Bran Nue Day　*Jimmy Chi* and
　Mick Manolis　97
We Are Going
　Oodgeroo Noonuccal　98
Whitefellas　*Post-Primary Boys'
　Class Papunya School*　99

Mimi Dancers
  Lorraine Mafi-Williams   100
The Curlew Cried
  Oodgeroo Noonuccal   101
Notes   102
Activities   103

The Oral Tradition   104

The 'word' of an antelope caught
  in a trap   *Sandag*   104
Leopard   *Yoruba poetry*   105
Three Songs from the Moon-Bone
  cycle   105
Notes   108
Activities   108

Poems and Pictures   109

The Cricketers   *Jeff Guess*   109
How to Paint the Portrait of a Bird
  Jacques Prévert   109
Giorgio de Chirico
  Philip Hodgins   111
Man Lying on a Wall
  Michael Longley   111
Paring the Apple
  Charles Tomlinson   112
Notes   113
Activities   116

Variations and Special Effects   117

Summary of a Western
  Sophie Hannah   117
The Horse That Had a Flat Tire
  Richard Brautigan   118
You'd Better Believe Him—A Fable
  Brian Patten   119
The Waiting Wolf   *Gwen Strauss*   119
Sleeping Snow-White
  Pamela Gillilan   121
The Other Version (1)
The Other Version (2)
  D. J. Enright   121

Nursery Rhyme of Innocence and
  Experience   *Charles Causley*   123
Notes   125
Activities   125

Readers' Theatre   127

Snake   *Brenton Mander*   127
The Alphabet Speaks Up!
  David Horner   128
Waltzing Matilda
  A. B. ('Banjo') Paterson   129
Leaves   *Ted Hughes*   130
Cicadas   *Paul Fleischman*   131
Notes   132
Activities   132

Close Ups   133

The Face of the Horse
  Nikolai Zabolotsky   134
At Grass   *Philip Larkin*   134
The Horses   *Ted Hughes*   135
Horses at Grass   *Leon Slade*   136
Notes   137
Activities   137

Reptilian Adventures   138

The Snake in the Department Store
  Philip Hodgins   138
Snake   *Emily Dickinson*   140
Forever the Snake
  Jennifer Rankin   141
Notes   142
Activities   142

Puzzles   143

Riddle   *John Birtwhistle*   143
Riddles   *John Fuller*   144
Snake Riddle   *Anon.*   144
Parable I   *Leo Aylen*   145
Notes   146
Activities   146

Ballads and Stories 147

The Streets of Laredo *Anon.* 147
Ballad *Gerda Mayer* 148
Unidentified Flying Object
   Robert Hayden 150
Faces in the Street *Henry Lawson* 152
What Has Happened to Lulu?
   Charles Causley 154
Song *Emily Brontë* 155
Notes 156
Activities 156

Perspectives 157

Stars *Paul B. Janeczko* 157

Assessment *Ted Kooser* 157
A Consumer's Report
   Peter Porter 158
When *Robert Zend* 159
Bury Me *Chu Hsiang* 160
Notes and Activities 161

Index of Titles and First Lines 163

Index of Poets 167

Acknowledgments 169

An Introduction to Reading and Teaching Poetry

The **Notes** and **Activities** are suggestions for making poems more accessible to students. They are likely to work best with students who work in an environment where they are used to, and value, the opportunity of writing and talking about their own work—including their own poetry. However, before we make suggestions about individual poems, we would like to make some general observations about reading and teaching poetry.

◆ Except in the case of the most transparent of narrative poems, a single reading of a poem is not enough. Before students are asked to discuss a poem they need time to become familiar with the poem by being given an opportunity to read the poem silently a couple of times, and to hear at least one, if not two, good readings by the teacher.

◆ Enjoyment of a poem is often deepened by close reading and analysis, but this does not mean line-by-line interrogation of a poem. Exercises of this nature are best avoided because they encourage students to see poetry lessons as a form of comprehension exercise carried out on language which doesn't say what it means. We need to discourage any message, implicit or explicit, which suggests that poetry is a foreign language needing to be translated by the teacher.

◆ A poem rarely 'belongs' to its reader on one or two readings, particularly when such readings are followed immediately by whole-class, question-and-answer discussion of an evaluative kind. 'Did you like that poem?' questions, and questions about diction, or rhyme patterns etc. are best deferred or not asked at all.

◆ Whether a poem is finally treasured or rejected, the teacher's role is to provide means for savouring and reflecting, bringing reader (or listener) and text closer together.

◆ Research has clearly demonstrated that the quality of whole-class discussion is greatly enhanced when the students have first been given the opportunity to discuss the poems in small groups.

◆ Rather than presenting a poem cold to students, who five minutes before may have been grappling with mathematics or biology, we urge teachers to provide a *context* in which a poem might be enriched and developed.

First Encounters with a Poem

◆ The students listen to a couple of readings of a poem and then quickly jot down their 'instant reactions' or 'first questions' in order to hold, discover, or begin to develop their own response.

◆ The teacher and class members who have prepared their readings read a new poem without discussion every day for a week. Closer exploration of some of these poems may follow.

◆ The teacher reserves part of the class-room display board for poems which are changed regularly. Keep those that have been on display in a file as part of the class's poetry resources. You could choose poems to match seasonal or topical events.

Sharing and Presenting Poems

◆ In pairs or groups, students work out ways of presenting different poems in dramatic form to the rest of the class.

◆ In pairs or groups, students prepare their own readings of the same poem (or put them on tape). The whole class listens, compares, discusses the similarities and differences.

◆ Groups make taped 'anthologies', perhaps with sound effects or music, which are exchanged with a parallel class.

◆ The teacher directs a whole-class choral reading, using a tape recorder in rehearsal, to foster the class's critical awareness and interpretation of the poem.

◆ Students choose photographs, slides or pictures to 'match' and accompany poems chosen for a poetry reading.

◆ Students illustrate narrative or episodic poems (e.g. ballads) and display them in a frieze or collate them in a loose-leaf folder. Each group illustrates a section of the poem with the text written beneath. Bind these together into a class anthology.

Becoming Familiar with a Poem

◆ Students could memorise a favourite poem. The choice should be personal, and might lead to a poem 'concert' but should never be the basis for a test.

Exploring a Poem to Increase Understanding and Appreciation

◆ Group discussion, with and without a guiding framework, is a most useful first step in exploring the dimensions of a poem, and for generating questions.

◆ In pairs, students write 'instant response' papers on a particular poem, exchange them and add comments to each other's responses before discussing them together.

◆ The teacher gives an untitled poem to a class. In pairs students propose a title, leading possibly to a final class consensus. The poet's original title is then considered, compared and discussed.

◆ As a way of exploring the structure of a poem, pairs or groups are presented with segments of the poem and place them in what they judge to be the right order. Discussion follows when the students' decisions are matched with the poet's.

◆ Students compare earlier drafts of a poet's work with the poet's final version (examples include poems by Wilfred Owen, Seamus Heaney, Judith Wright). Discussion follows when the students' decisions are matched with the poet's.

◆ Students model, imitate, parody, or construct a pastiche of a particular poem, groups of poems, technique, or form. (See the Multiple Exposures and Portraits sections of this book.)

◆ Borrow some of the techniques for exploring prose narratives: invent the story behind the poem: what has happened before? what is happening 'off-stage'? what might happen next?

◆ In groups of up to four, students decide on the key word or line in the poem.

Asking Questions

◆ Using large sheets of paper, groups prepare factual questions (or question webs) as a way into a poem, and use these as the basis for a whole-class exploration.

◆ Groups or pairs prepare open-ended 'response' questions on matters of opinion about the poem. (Avoid 'Do you like this poem?' It probably won't lead anywhere.)

◆ Individuals, or groups, prepare their own questions which they need to ask the teacher.

Demystifying

◆ Invite a published poet to your school to read and talk about his/her work. (Some schools have poet-in-residence programs.)

◆ Encourage students to see themselves as poetry writers.

Knowing When to Move On

◆ Persevering with a poem disliked by a class, even after it has had a fair hearing, seems counter-productive. Negative responses (when informed) need to be expressed and respected.

Studying the Craft and Techniques of Poetry

◆ For the skilled poetry lover, using literary terminology acts as a useful tool and as a shorthand for exposing the way a poem 'works'; for the student, it is a

new vocabulary that may get in the way of a natural responsiveness to patterns, images and rhythms.

Are there ways of preventing (or minimising) alienation? We would encourage students to experiment with, and craft language; and to see themselves as authors of poems or poetic constructs—not simply passive receivers of the Great Works of Dead Poets.

Useful teachers' reference books on poetry include: Richard Andrews *The Problem with Poetry* (Open University, 1991); Michael Benton and Geoff Fox *Teaching Literature, Nine to Fourteen* (Oxford University Press, 1985); Mike Hayhoe and Stephen Parker *Words Large as Apples* (Cambridge University Press, 1988); Bill Corcoran and Emrys Evans (eds) *Readers, Texts, Teachers* (Boynton/Cook Heinemann, 1987).

A Note on Readers' Theatre

The oral side of poetry seems to be largely neglected in the middle and senior secondary years, perhaps because adolescents, unless they have had positive experiences in the earlier years of schooling, react against the idea of choral speaking. This is the more unfortunate because most poetry is meant to be heard as well as read.

We have found that at this level readers' theatre is the ideal way of restoring the oral dimension to poetry. Students, in small groups, take twenty minutes or so to decide how a particular poem can be presented to the class. Remind them that some lines or phrases might be said by the whole group, some by two voices, some by a single voice. They also need to decide questions of tone and emphasis. After a couple of practice runs they can provide a book-in-hand reading that brings out their interpretation of the poem.

Poems in this collection well suited to readers' theatre include: *Stop All the Clocks* by W. H. Auden (page 55), *The Song of the Whale* by Kit Wright (page 43).

Paul Fleischman's *Cicadas*, a poem for two voices, will need some practice, as when the two readers have lines printed on the same horizontal level they must read them simultaneously. Fleischman has published two collections of dialogue poems: *Joyful Noise* (HarperCollins, 1988) and *I Am Phoenix* (HarperCollins, 1985). In 1989 *Joyful Noise* won the Newbery Medal awarded annually to the author of the most distinguished contribution to American children's literature.

For more on oral presentation, teachers will find *A Book to Perform Poems By* by Rory Harris and Peter McFarlane (AATE, 1985) useful. *Postcards from Planet Earth*, the companion volume to *Snapshots of Planet Earth*, also contains poems suitable for readers' theatre.

Words

Snapshots

My poems are snapshots.

They catch

the moment's truth only.

Tomorrow my mood

will blow from a different quarter;

bend the facts

another way.

Gerda Mayer
[British]

The title for this anthology and many of the poems included in it had already been selected when we received Gerda Mayer's poem **'Snapshots'**. Her poem aptly captures the way some poets work and mirrors the way in which we have collected these poems providing the perfect introduction to this anthology.

Gerda Mayer was born in Czechoslovakia but was brought to England as a child.

Words

They are stones
shaped to the hand.
Fling them accurately.

They are horses.
Bridle them;
they'll run away with you.

They are windows,
opening on vistas
that are unreachable.

They are apples.
Bite on hardness
to the sweet core.

They are coracles;
flimsy,
soon overloaded.

They are candles.
Carry them carefully.
They have buried cities.

Catherine Fisher
[British]

Consumer Poems

conform to safety standards, have been rigorously checked,
are guaranteed free from deleterious side-effects,
will not harm pregnant women or play havoc with your
    purse,
leave children of all ages and both sexes none the worse,
won't remove your eyebrows, spoil your nails or aggravate
skin complaints and dandruff; are no danger to the State.
They're washable, unbreakable, hygenic, well designed,
non-iron, non-crease, non-toxic, non-inflammable, non-
    aligned.

But beware of imitations which have recently come to light,
inferior products marketed subversively at night.
Innocuous though they may at first appear, don't be
    deceived —
they are the work of undesirable elements, aggrieved
by lack of status or comfort: men who listen to the tides,
memorize the workings of flowers and loiter at the roadside
Leave dangerous poems such as these unread — or else, by
    stealth,
a sense of hope could once again damage the national
    health.

Lawrence Sail *[British]*

The Television Poem

(for Patrick Taggart)

It is midnight.
You are passing the window
of a television showroom —
the door is barred,
a wire grille is in the window.
The shop is closed.

This poem is being transmitted to you
from inside the television showroom.
This poem comes to you twice in colour,
twice in black and white.
This poem is 625 lines.
This poem is 21 inches
across the diagonal.

You do not hear this poem —
for all you know
this poem could be forecasting ice.
This poem could be telling of the world's end.
This poem could, conceivably,
be singing.

You will see this poem
but will fail to recognise it.
You will not hear this poem
without straining to hear it.
This poem is a mouth opening and closing
and opening and closing
and opening. O.

This poem is subliminal —
dismiss it.
This poem is ephemeral
and eminently passable.
Pass this poem —
let the poem be.

This poem is not for you.
This is my poem,
it is private.
Do not halt in your tracks for this poem.
Go about your business.
See her home.
See yourself home.

You will go home, together or alone.
You will sleep, together or alone.
In the morning you will awaken
and will forget every word of this poem.
There is nothing to remember.
There is nothing to forget.

You will not hear this poem.
This happens to most poems.

Pete Morgan
[British]

Pencil

Someone writes with me
his fingers clutch my waist
he holds me tight leads me on
holds me tight again

The poem done he drops me
I feel diminished
and with surprise I read
the part of me he wore away

Robert Zend
[Hungarian]

Thunderstorms

My mind has thunderstorms,
    That brood for heavy hours:
Until they rain me words,
    My thoughts are drooping flowers
And sulking silent birds.

Yet come, dark thunderstorms,
    And brood your heavy hours;
For when you rain me words,
    My thoughts are dancing flowers
And joyful singing birds.

W. H. Davies
[British]

Living Language

How many sentences wander each day
past my retreat?
I am too scared to come and entertain them
    with some street-corner conversation,
    tying words in shallow parcels
    and expecting a full stop to every question mark.
How many questions remain unanswered till eternity
because of all the hermits of conversation who live
crablike in shallow water?
Try to catch the exclamation mark
with the millions of smiles and tears.
Place it in front of our eyes and
guard its form, so it does not bend to query.

Jane Donald
[Australian]

Notes

Catherine Fisher, a Welsh poet, tells us how powerful yet fragile words can be; while Lawrence Sail, an English poet, reminds us how easy it is to debase language. Pete Morgan has said that 'The Television Poem' was written after he had, late one night in the English town of Swindon, passed a television showroom where four television sets in the window were showing the same picture. 'On each screen the same person was blabbing about something or other but I couldn't hear a word.'

'Pencil'

For most writers, 'trying to get the better of words' is a constant struggle. Occasionally, however, writers have a different experience. Ivan Southall, a well-known writer for young people, has said that he often feels that 'someone up there' is writing his novels for him. Robert Zend's 'Pencil' gives poetic expression to such an experience.

'Thunderstorms'

In this poem, W. H. Davies draws our attention to the fact that language and thought are not identical, but it is language that gives life to our thoughts. The Russian psychologist Lev Vygotsky, in his book *Thought and Language* included a quote from a Russian poem that applies here:

> I have forgotten the word I intended to say, and my thought, unembodied, returns to the realm of shadows.

'Living Language'

Jane Donald was an Australian school student when she wrote 'Living Language', in which she testifies, in a series of powerful images, to the difficulties we all have with language.

Activities

◆ What kind of society would produce 'consumer poems'? Can you pick out the advertising clichés? As you read the poems in *Snapshots of Planet Earth*, watch out for some of the 'dangerous poems' that the narrating voice, a sort of 'Big Brother', warns against.

◆ Before 'The Television Poem' is read, imagine yourself in the situation that led Pete Morgan to write his poem. Write down your reactions as you gaze into the shop window. Then, after the poem has been read two or three times by your teacher, you could, in your group, try to decide what the poet really feels. Is he commenting on how what we see on television is so quickly forgotten? Is he using the scene as a metaphor for the difficulty the poet has in reaching an audience? Is he asserting that the poet is simply writing for himself?

◆ In small groups, discuss **'Thunderstorms'** and **'Living Language'**, sharing your thoughts about the difficulties of communication—particularly those occasions when language seems to have failed.

Action Shots

Snap Shot

He's on your hammer, closing in with every bounce
pushing you deeper and deeper into the pocket,
the gap between the goalposts closing fast,
as fast as other options are running out.
Your only choice is to try the Snap.
Holding the ball at either end
just like the umpire does
you screw it sideways
inside the line
and watch it
lucklessly
hit the
post.

Philip Hodgins
[*Australian*]

Drop Kick

The noblest Kick that ever left a boot.
It had a different flight to most of them
because it started off from lower down
just at the point it lifted off the turf
which meant you kicked it with a fuller arc
increasing Power without a loss of Grace.
Of course this made a few demands on Skill:
you had to drop the ball more carefully,
it took a moment longer to perform,
and if you didn't judge it well enough
the ball would only grub along the ground;
or if your game was going really wrong
you'd stub your toes or even break your foot.
The risks were just as great as the rewards.

A Kick like this, with all of life at stake,
could never be expected to survive
in what became a game for money men.

They forced it out because it took too long
(therefore returns could never be as quick)
and even more importantly because
you can't invest in something so unsure.
They didn't care about the spectacle,
the past, or what elliptic scope there was.
The coaches passed the business message on
and players slowly, sadly, changed their game.
The last reported Drop Kick in the League
was at the 'G' about four years ago.
In time-on, with his team down fifty points,
when all was lost, a youngster let one go,
believing it was just a bit of fun.
Before the ball had landed he was dragged.

Philip Hodgins
[Australian]

Place Kick

Still somewhere in the rule-book
    but like
    a bunyip
existing only in the old stories.
    Not one
    live fan
has seen them in the solid hide.
    They are
    as clumsy
and as antiquated as the dinosaur
    but they
    ave not
become extinct like that creature.
    They are
    in hiding
until the game has evolved enough
    for them
    to come
and take their place among Kicks,
    the lowest
    of the low
still able to keep their head up.

Philip Hodgins
[Australian]

Junior Coaching

Throw the ball up. Try to whack it
  over the net and in that square.
No no, Fiona! With the racquet!
  Tom, stop pulling Janet's hair.
Yes, Dave, racquets cost a packet
  Oh, your dad's a millionaire.

That's all right then. What's his swindle?
  No, Tom, you can't smash just yet.
When you're tall and tough as Lendl . . .
  Darren, don't let down that net!
Now girls, who said you could spend all
  afternoon tormenting Brett?

Watch the ball! Turn! Arm back early!
  Bend your knees, and follow through!
Just like this. Look. Oh, well nearly.
  Now let's see what you can do.
Well done, Kimberley! You've clearly
  volleyed that to Timbuctoo!

Dave, I think your track suit's smashing.
  Yes, I like the headband too.
You've got the gear, you've got the passion,
  just like teenage McEnroe.
Now hit the ball, and try to ration
  all the things your mouth can do.

Pick up balls, please! Come on, quickly!
  Balls to me! Now who threw that?
Kimberley, you look quite sickly.
  What? You've lost your new school hat?
Thank you, Darren. Yes, it's triff'ckly
  tightly strung, your Becker bat.

Quiet! QUIET! Thanks a million.
Got *all* your stuff? See you next week.
Kate, you may. In the pavilion.
Well, there goes the nation's freak-
y, cheeky, whacky, billion brill ones
piping homeward, in the peak!

William Scammell
[British]

The Surf-Rider

Out in the Golfe de Gascogne, on the far
edge of the Atlantic beside Biarritz,
the surf-rider surfaces from a trough
in the sea's swell, seeming to pull at the reins
of air currents while the wave wheels him
as on a chariot, the horses of momentum,
harnessed to wind, throwing back manes of sea-spray:

When the wave's swelling explodes in a dust-
storm of surf with a crowd-roar in the bay's
amphitheatre of tiers of the tide's coming,
he wobbles a moment as in a rut, then,
leaning into the wind, arms loosening,
makes the surf as firm as cobblestones, his
heels as secure as iron rims on wheels:

And now he rides the ocean, conqueror
of air and water in a contest of force,
heeling above the lion's pit of depth:
until the surf eases, reaches the shore,
dragging him down to his knees. The illusion,
that a god had risen from the ocean
and miraculously walked upon the water breaks.

Zulfikar Ghose
[Pakistani]

The Surfer

He thrust his joy against the weight of the sea;
climbed through, slid under those long banks of
 foam —
(hawthorn hedges in spring, thorns in the face stinging).
How his brown strength drove through the hollow and coil
of green-through weirs of water!
Muscle of arm thrust down long muscle of water;
and swimming so, went out of sight
where mortal, masterful, frail, the gulls went wheeling
in air as he in water, with delight.
Turn home, the sun goes down; swimmer, turn home.
Last leaf of gold vanishes from the sea-curve.
Take the big roller's shoulder, speed and swerve;
come to the long beach home like a gull diving.

For on the sand the grey-wolf sea lies snarling,
cold twilight wind splits the waves' hair and shows
the bones they worry in their wolf-teeth. O, wind blows
and sea crouches on sand, fawning and mouthing;
drop there and snatches again, drops and again snatches
its broken toys, its whitened pebbles and shells.

Judith Wright
[Australian]

First Fight

I
Tonight, then, is the night;
Stretched on the massage table,
Wrapped in his robe, he breathes
Liniment and sweat
And tries to close his ears
To the roaring of the crowd,
A mirky sea of noise
That bears upon its tide
The frail sound of the bell
And brings the cunning fear
That he might not do well.
Not fear of bodily pain
But that his tight-lipped pride
Might be sent crashing down,
His white ambition slain,
Knocked spinning the glittering crown.
How could his spirit bear

That ignonimous fall?
Not hero but a clown
Spurned or scorned by all.
The thought appals, and he
Feels sudden envy for
The roaring crowd outside
And wishes he were there
Anonymous and safe,
Calm in the tolerant air,
Would almost choose to be
Anywhere but here.

II
The door blares open suddenly,
The room is sluiced with row;
His second says, "We're on next fight,
We'd better get going now.
You got your gumshield, haven't you?
Just loosen up—that's right—
Don't worry, boy, you'll be okay
Once you start to fight."
Out of the dressingroom, along,
The neutral passage to
The yelling cavern where the ring
Through the haze of blue
Tobacco smoke is whitewashed by
The aching glare of light:
Geometric ropes are stretched as taut
As this boy's nerves are tight.

And now he's in his corner where
He tries to look at ease;
He feels the crowd's sharp eyes as they
Prick and pry and tease;
He hears them murmur like the sea
Or some great dynamo:
They are not hostile yet they wish
To see his lifeblood flow.

His adversary enters now;
The boy risks one quick glance;
He does not see an enemy
But something there by chance,
Not human even, but a cold
Abstraction to defeat,
A problem to be solved by guile,
Quick hands and knowing feet.
The fighters' names are shouted out;
They leave their corners for

The touch of gloves and brief commands;
The disciplines of war.
Back in their corners, stripped of robes,
They hear the bell clang *one*
Brazen syllable which says
The battle has begun.

You're moving smooth and confident
In comfortable gear.
Jab with the left again,
Quickly move away;
Feint and stab another in,
See him duck and sway.
Now for the pay-off punch,
Smash it hard inside;
It thuds against his jaw, he falls,
Limbs spread wide.
And suddenly you hear the roar,
Hoarse music of the crowd,
Voicing your hot ecstasy,
Triumphant, male, and proud.

III
Bite on gumshield,
Guard held high,
The crowd are silenced,
All sounds die.
Lead with the left,
Again, again;
Watch for the opening,
Feint and then
Hook to the body
But he's blocked it and
Slammed you back
With a fierce right hand.
Hang on grimly,
The fog will clear,
Sweat in your nostrils,
Grease and fear.
You're hurt and staggering,
Shocked to know
That the story's altered:
He's the hero!

But the mist is clearing,
The referee snaps
A rapid warning
And he smartly taps

Your hugging elbow
And then you step back
Ready to counter
The next attack,
But the first round finishes
Without mishap.
You suck in the air
From the towel's skilled flap.
A voice speaks urgently
Close to your ear:
"Keep your left going, boy,
Stop him getting near.
He wants to get close to you,
So jab him off hard;
When he tries to slip below,
Never mind your guard,
Crack him with a solid right,
Hit him on the chin,
A couple downstairs
And then he'll pack it in."

Slip in the gumshield
Bite on it hard,
Keep him off with your left,
Never drop your guard.
Try a left hook,
But he crosses with a right
Smack on your jaw
And Guy Fawkes Night
Flashes and dazzles
Inside your skull,
Your knees go bandy
And you almost fall.
Keep the left jabbing,
Move around the ring,
Don't let him catch you with
Another hook or swing.
Keep your left working,
Keep it up high,
Stab it out straight and hard,
Again—above the eye.
Sweat in the nostrils,
But nothing now of fear.

IV
Now, in the sleepless darkness of his room
The boy, in bed, remembers. Suddenly
The victory tastes sour. The man he fought

Was not a thing, as lifeless as a broom,
He was a man who hoped and trembled too;
What of him now? What was *he* going through?
And then the boy bites hard on resolution:
Fighters can't pack pity with their gear,
And yet a bitter taste stays with the notion;
He's forced to swallow down one treacherous tear.
But that's the last. He is a boy no longer;
He is a man, a fighter, such as jeer
At those who make salt beads with melting eyes,
Whatever might cry out, is hurt, or dies.

Vernon Scannell
[British]

𝒩otes

'Snap Shot', 'Drop Kick' and 'Place Kick' all refer to Australian Rules Football. Like many Australians, Hodgins was devoted to the game.

'Snap Shot'
on your hammer—a colloquial phrase meaning that someone is very close behind you
the pocket—a term referring to a field position

'Drop Kick'
drop kick—a kick in which the ball is dropped from the hands of the player towards the turf and makes contact with the boot just as it comes off the ground. It still features in both Rugby League and Rugby Union football.
the G—the Melbourne Cricket Ground, which is considered by many to be the 'home' of Australian Rules Football

'Place Kick'
place kick—the ball is placed on the ground, usually on a small mound of earth, and is kicked into the air in the direction of the goal posts. The kick is still used in Rugby League and Rugby Union football.

Philip Hodgins was born at Shepparton, Victoria, in 1958 and grew up on a dairy farm. After some years of living in the city, he returned to the country with his wife and two children. He lived in central Victoria near Maryborough and died from leukaemia in 1995 aged thirty-six. His poems often reveal his affection for country life and country people. Other poems by Philip Hodgins appear on pages 46, 111 and 138.

'Junior Coaching'
This poem is by English poet William Scammell whose collection *The Game* (Peterloo Poets) explores many aspects of tennis.

Ivan Lendl—an international tennis star who resides in the USA. He was famous for his well-timed groundstokes.

McEnroe—John McEnroe, a temperamental US tennis star of considerable ability who became famous for his on-court tantrums

Becker—Boris Becker, a German tennis star who won Wimbledon at the age of 17

'The Surf-Rider'
Golfe de Gascogne—part of the French coast in the region of Gascogne

Biarritz—a French resort town close to the border between France and Spain, on the Cote d'Argent where the Atlantic Ocean forms the Bay of Biscay

Poseidon—In Greek mythology Zeus was considered to be the presiding deity of the universe, the god who controlled the forces of nature and the existence of men. His brother Poseidon was made ruler of the seas by Zeus. Poseidon, often depicted riding horses across the waves, was also called 'the earthshaker' because he had the power to create storms and volcanic eruptions.

'The Surfer'

Judith Wright is one of Australia's best known living poets. She was born in 1915 into a pioneering family in New England and has long been an activist for Aboriginal rights. Her work includes a range of other literature besides poetry. Wright often explores aspects of the natural world as metaphors for asking questions about the meaning of existence and humanity. The last stanza of Wright's poem when compared with Edward Lowbury's 'Breakers' (page 44) could promote an interesting discussion of the way poets create and use metaphor. (See also **Notes** and **Activities** on pages 39 to 40 for further suggestions concerning the use of metaphor.)

'First Fight'

Vernon Scannell, an English poet, was a professional boxer before becoming a freelance writer. George Orwell's essay *The Sporting Spirit* could be read in conjunction with **'First Fight'**. The poem draws on the ballad tradition by telling a simple story in verse. (See the Ballads and Stories Section for examples of other ballads.)

Activities

Using **'Junior Coaching'** as a model, see if you can write a poem in which you include the names of your friends. You might also like to adapt Scammell's poem so that it refers to a sport other than tennis.

Multiple Exposures

Thirteen Ways of Looking at a Blackbird

I
Among twenty snowy mountains,
The only moving thing
Was the eye of the blackbird.

II
I was of three minds,
Like a tree
In which there are three blackbirds.

III
The blackbird whirled in the autumn winds.
It was a small part of the pantomime.

IV
A man and a woman
Are one.
A man and a woman and a blackbird.
Are one.

V
I do not know which to prefer,
The beauty of inflections
Or the beauty of innuendoes,
The blackbird whistling
Or just after.

VI
Icicles filled the long window
With barbaric glass.
The shadow of the blackbird
Crossed it, to and fro.
The mood
Traced in the shadow
An indecipherable cause.

VII
O thin men of Haddam,
Why do you imagine golden birds?
Do you not see how the blackbird
Walks around the feet
Of the women about you?

VIII
I know noble accents
And lucid, inescapable rhythms;
But I know, too,
That the blackbird is involved
In what I know.

IX
When the blackbird flew out of sight,
It marked the edge
Of one of many circles.

X
At the sight of blackbirds
Flying in a green light,
Even the bawds of euphony
Would cry out sharply.

XI
He rode over Connecticut
In a glass coach.
Once, a fear pierced him,
In that he mistook
The shadow of his equipage
For blackbirds.

XII
The river is moving.
The blackbird must be flying.

XIII
It was evening all afternoon.
It was snowing
And it was going to snow.
The blackbird sat
In the cedar-limbs.

Wallace Stevens
[USA]

Thirteen Ways of Looking at a Blackboard

I
The blackboard is clean.
The master must be coming.

II
The vigilant mosquito bites on a rising pitch.
The chalk whistles over the blackboard.

III
Among twenty silent children
The only moving thing
Is the chalk's white finger.

IV
O young white cricketers,
Aching for the greensward,
Do you not see how my moving hand
Whitens the black board?

V
A man and a child
Are one.
A man and a child and a blackboard
Are three.

VI
Some wield their sticks of chalk
Like torches in dark rooms.
I make up my blackboard
Like the face of an actor.

VII
I was of three minds
Like a room
In which there are three blackboards.

VIII
I dream
I am an albino.

IX
I wake.
I forget a word.
The chalk snaps on the blackboard.

X
Twenty silent children
Staring at the blackboard.
On one wall of each of twenty nurseries
The light has gone out.

XI
He ambles along the white rocks of Dover,
Crushing pebbles with black boots.
He is a small blackboard
Writing on chalk.

XII
It is the Christmas holidays.
The white snow lies in the long black branches.
The black board
In the silent schoolroom
Perches on two stubby branches.

XIII
The flesh that is white
Wastes over the bones that are chalk,
Both in the day
And through the black night.

Peter Redgrove
[British]

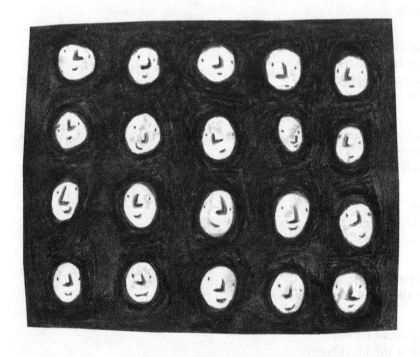

Fourteen Ways of Touching the Peter

I
You can push
your thumb
in the
ridge
between his
shoulder-blades
to please him.

II
Starting
at its root,
you can let
his whole
tail
flow
through your hand.

III
Forming
a fist
you can let
him rub
his bone
skull
against it, hard.

IV
When he makes
bread,
you can lift
him
by his under
sides on your
knuckles.

V
In hot
weather
you can itch
the fur
under
his chin. He
likes that.

VI
At night
you can hoist
him
out of his bean-stalk,
sleepily
clutching
paper bags.

VII
Pressing
his head against
your cheek,
you can carry
him
in the dark,
safely.

VIII
In late Autumn
you can find
seeds
adhering
to his fur.
There are
plenty.

IX
You can prise
his jaws
open,
helping
any medicine
he won't
abide, go down.

X
You can touch
his
feet, only
if
he is relaxed.
He
doesn't like it.

XI
You can comb
spare thin
fur
from his coat,
so he won't
get
fur-ball.

XII
You can shake
his rigid
chicken-leg leg,
scouring his
hind-quarters
with his Vim
tongue.

XIII
Dumping
hot fish
on his plate, you can
fend
him off,
pushing
and purring

XIV
You can have
him shrimp
along you,
breathing,
whenever
you want
to compose poems.

George MacBeth
[British]

The Red Wheelbarrow

so much depends
upon

a red wheel
barrow

glazed with rain
water

beside the white
chickens

William Carlos Williams
[USA]

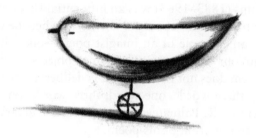

The Poem William Carlos Williams
Never Wrote But Might Have,
Had He Lived on Mangoes for a Year

nothing depends
upon

a blood red
mango

sliced into
bits

upon bone white
china.

R. Palmateer
[USA]

Notes

Wallace Stevens, a major US poet, certainly started something when he decided to write a poem which 'looked' at something from several different angles.

Clearly, Peter Redgrove had Stevens' poem in mind when he wrote **'Thirteen Ways of Looking at a Blackboard'**, and so did George MacBeth when he wrote his poem about 'the Peter' (his cat—known as the Peter because he was unique—like the Pope!). Although the first two poems are richer in imagery, MacBeth is more tightly constructed, as there are fourteen words in each section. The most striking feature of Redgrove's poem is the manner in which it manages to create its meaning. Each of the thirteen stanzas provides a single frame or image which is self-contained, and yet as we move through the poem we carry the impression left by the preceding stanza. It might be worth considering whether the 'I' of stanzas VI, VII, VIII and IX is the one persona.

William Carlos Williams (1883–1963) was an influential US poet. He spent his life working as a pediatrician in the town in New Jersey where he was born. **'The Red Wheelbarrow'** is an example of an imagist poem—one which creates an image which enters into our 'mind's eye'. The named objects are drawn together by association. The poem does not rhyme, yet it is deliberately constructed into seven lines alternating three words, one word, three words, one word, and so on. Although the poem by R. Palmateer alters the line structure employed by Williams, it is clearly an imitation of his poem.

Activities

◆ This section provides some useful models for your own writing. Take another common object and develop a series of images suggested by it, as in the first three poems.

◆ Try to write an imagist poem in the manner of William Carlos Williams. Close your eyes and concentrate on an image you can recall. Then try to write your poem by starting with:

So much depends
upon . . .

Follow exactly the line pattern of the Williams poem (a seven line poem in which a three-word line alternates with a one-word line).

Portraits

Car Salesman

Framed in his showroom, tinted and furbished well—
A slide projected on the plastic wall—
The salesman hangs in wait to sell;

Till the buyer's tread, like a button touched or bell rung,
Signalling animation, jerks him to life,
Unwinds the message taped across his tongue;

Minces and mimics, hides a youth's pink pride,
And, lubricated with hypocrisy,
Insists on taking madame for a ride.

Row on row the new cars snarl and grin
Behind him—crouched, obsequious, and yet
With quiet irony content to hem him in.

Their pulsing synthesis of pipes and pistons, thrust and curled
In steel, remain no more insensitive than he,
Poor nerveless puppet of the brave new world;

Effete and unaware, he helps traduce
His heart; sells car and birthright glibly. On the wall
A graph like a whiplash bends him to its use.

He and his product from the same production line,
Ducoed with gloss, pretension and conceit,
Both advertise the altars of our time.

Colin Thiele
[Australian]

from The Canterbury Tales

The MILLERE was a stout carl for the nones;
Full byg he was of brawn, and eek of bones.
That proved wel, for over al ther he cam,
At wrastlynge he wolde have alwey the ram.
He was short-sholdred, brood, a thikke knarre;
Ther was no dore that he nolde heve at harre,
Or breke it at a rennyng with his heed.
His berd as any sowe or fox was reed,
And therto brood, as though it were a spade.
Upon the cop right of his nose he hade
A werte, and theron stood a toft of herys,
Reed as the brustles of a sowes erys;
His nosethirles blake were and wyde.
A swerd and bokeler bar he by his syde.
His mouth as greet was as a greet forneys.
He was a janglere and a goliardeys,
And that was moost of synne and harlotries.
Wel koude he stelen corn and tollen thries;
And yet he hadde a thombe of gold, pardee.
A whit cote and a blew hood wered he.
A baggepipe wel koude he blowe and sowne,
And therwithal he broghte us out of towne.

Geoffrey Chaucer
[English]

from The Cantbeworried Tales

An ADVERTISING AGENT with us ther
Al sharpely was arrayed with crewe-cut hayre,
Gygantik blak-framed glasses, snap-brimme hat
and Pinke stryped shirts with collar buttoned flat.
A wel-cut charcoal suit did hugge his jointes.
And on his feete Italian Shoon with pointes.
'One tyme,' syede hee, 'wordes were my cheefe concern:
For clients I with verbal zeale wolde burn
To crack my braines for one compellying phrase
That wolde reluctaunt customers amaze.
All goodes were fabulous or elles unique
And fresshe superlatives wer harde to seeke.
Then Motivational Researche bigan
With analytick subtiltee to scan
Unconscious weaknesses, and flaws and quirks–
And so confirmed my faithe and blest my workes.

I sel nat soap to girles, I sel Romance;
I sel Virilitee, nat young mennes pantes.
Som brandes of cigarettes as yow may gesse
Give promise of executive success;
With sondree othre brandes eche puff of smoke
Wil make yow strong and handsome outdoor folke.
But tho my methods have a different name,
The facts aboute mankind remayn the same;
For eche man is a vayn and greedye snob.
If this wer false, I wolde nat have a job.'
How trew, methinks, and yet what kinde of man
Wil get his joy exployting where hee can
Folkes common faultes? Perhaps withinne his soule
A gross of gimmicks fils a gaping hole.

... A man ther was who handled REAL ESTATE;
To fil his car hee did nat hesitate
With familyes al anxious to inspecte
The bargains in his boke; tho to protect
Upholsteree from litel children's feete
Hee hadde with plastick covered every seate.
And charmed hee folke with Dale Carnegie loke
and flicked the pages of his listings-boke
So ful, if semed the whole worlde wished to sel;
Yet anyone that glanced thereinne colde tel
Som pages emptee wer, some entrees olde
And som at half the price colde nat bee solde.
His talentyd performance startes I gesse
With advertysng in the dailee presse;
A HOUSE OF CHARACTER yow reade, but finde
Hee never semes to specifye what kinde;
From house with views yow mighte with goode luck see
The topmoste branches of a distaunt tree;
PLEASANTLY ELEVATED—yes, on rocke—
To climbe therto yow neede an alpenstocke;
and FOUR BEDROOM ACCOMM. meanes yow must scrounge
Som extra space from dinyng-roome and lounge;
not a penny to spend—wel ther are groundes
For honestee: yow spend nat pence but poundes;
IDEAL FOR HANDYMAN—This one's for chappes
whose skil postpones its imminent collapse.
No lies tels hee; but does the trewthe conceale;
Thus al Estate hee sels is nat quite Real.

David Swain
[Australian]

Perfect Beggar

He squats beside an antique sewing-machine
outside the Asian store and frankly waits
for us and as we near, his face divides
like a wrinkled pod disclosing broken teeth:
an almost happy smile. And then he thrusts
the scabby knobs of leprous hands towards
your purse, as if he had some rather old
potatoes to dispose of, smiles and trusts
that you will see the meaning of his stumps:
a man who has no fingers *cannot* work,
must therefore beg. And he's content while
ten other men nearby in idle clumps
wait sour and silent, their workless fingers jammed
deep down their empty pockets.

David Gill
[British]

The Angry Man

The other day I chanced to meet
An angry man upon the street—
A man of wrath, a man of war,
A man who truculently bore
Over his shoulder, like a lance,
A banner labeled "Tolerance."

And when I asked him why he strode
Thus scowling down the human road,
Scowling, he answered, "I am he
Who champions total liberty—
Intolerance being, ma'am, a state
No tolerant man can tolerate.

"When I meet rogues," he cried, "who choose
To cherish oppositional views,
Lady, like this, and in this manner,
I lay about me with my banner
Till they cry mercy, ma'am." His blows
Rained proudly on prospective foes.

Fearful, I turned and left him there
Still muttering, as he thrashed the air,
"Let the Intolerant beware!"

Phyllis McGinley
[USA]

Simply Being Jim

(for L.M.)

When you land in the bush
there's always a man
waiting
in a hat.
He leans on a gate
as you taxi
through the dust
at Walgett or Narrabri
until you enter his perspective
then
he eases upright
and grins.
He's Jim
   he says
casually
offering a hand.
If you mention
the weather
or the hard season
he'll agree affably.
He'll drive
the regulation mile
to "The Palms" motel
in an off-white ute
with a brown dog
in the back
and should you speak
again
he will answer.

Tomorrow
he'll see you off
and lean on the gate

Later
he'll meet you
at Stanthorpe or Bourke.

Ian Saw
[Australian]

Warning

When I am an old woman I shall wear purple
With a red hat which doesn't go, and doesn't suit me,
And I shall spend my pension on brandy and summer gloves
And satin sandals, and say we've no money for butter.
I shall sit down on the pavement when I am tired
And gobble up samples in shops and press alarm bells
And run my stick along the public railings
And make up for the sobriety of my youth.
I shall go out in my slippers in the rain
And pick the flowers in other people's gardens
And learn to spit.

You can wear terrible shirts and grow more fat
And eat three pounds of sausages at a go
Or only bread and pickle for a week
And hoard pens and pencils and beermats and things in boxes.

But now we must have clothes that keep us dry
And pay our rent and not swear in the street
And set a good example for the children.
We will have friends to dinner and read the papers.

But maybe I ought to practise a little now?
So people who know me are not too shocked and surprised
When suddenly I am old and start to wear purple.

Jenny Joseph
[British]

'Ghost Wanted; Young, Willing'

Dear Sir,
With reference to yours of the 7th inst.,
I wish to apply for the vacancy
Faith or requited love has created in your staff.
The following are my qualifications: namely,
A dozen years in various threadbare lodgings,
Which have sharpened a doubtless natural melancholy
To that point of keenness where it need but little
Time to adapt itself to the particular
Idiosyncrasies of bad plumbing and worn stairs . . .

It might be as well to mention at this juncture
That over this period I have acquired the necessary
Sense of impermanence without which
No prospective ghost can make his way in the world,
Having studied, to this end, in sundry dwellings,
The alluvial deposits of past species
(Hair-pins and empty scent-bottles, and on walls
The pencilling of long-disconnected telephone numbers);
And, pressing cold lips to jaundiced mirrors, found there
(As with the dead) no momentary clouding.

In addition, I must state that in the field
Of practical experience I have eaten
A thousand meals in bright fly-spotted cafés,
Sharing my morsel of pathos with a throng
Of vacant-eyed habitués, where the only
Thing that is substantial is the bill,
And drawn by the blind nickel-and-chrome benevolence
Of cinema foyers, watched my flickering counterparts
Live out their depthless lives, while lovers mocked
Their phantasms from the true world of the stalls.

In closing I assure you that should this
Application be successful I will prove
Most satisfactory in whatever post
You choose to place me,
                               bearing in mind, of course
That, being by nature still a mere apprentice,
Only you, Death, can make me journeyman . . .

Bruce Dawe
[Australian]

 # Notes

'Car Salesman' is by the Australian poet Colin Thiele. David Swain, the author of *The Cantbeworried Tales*, is also an Australian, as is Bruce Dawe.

The description of the Miller from the Prologue to Chaucer's *The Canterbury Tales* needs to be read aloud before students will be able to appreciate fully the two selections from David Swain's *The Cantbeworried Tales*, which satirise various figures in modern society.

Phyllis McGinley was a very distinguished US practitioner of light verse, usually with a satirical twist.

 # Activities

◆ **'Car Salesman'** lends itself to narration as an accompaniment to a series of mimed scenarios.

◆ In your group, construct another portrait in the manner of *The Cantbeworried Tales*.

◆ John Clarke, the well known comedian and social commentator originally from New Zealand, has a collection of comic monologues on CD entitled *The Fred Dagg Tapes* (Festival Records D19742, 1992). One of the monologues deals with real estate and another with advertising, and these would pair well with David Swain's parodies. *The Cantbeworried Tales* and *The Fred Dagg Tapes* are good starting points for a close examination of the language and rhetorical strategies of advertising, particularly the uses of metaphor, connotative language and clichés (see later in this section An Activity on Clichés and Metaphoric Language).

◆ After reading **'Perfect Beggar'**, create a collage in a small group, of the many photographs of human distress that fill our newspapers and magazines, either as a background for presentation of the poem or as a stimulus for further writing on such themes.

◆ In 1996 the BBC conducted a poll amongst its radio listeners to determine the most popular modern poem: 7000 votes were received. Jenny Joseph's **'Warning'** won the most votes, followed by:

'Not Waving But Drowning'—Stevie Smith
'Do Not Go Gentle into That Good Night'—Dylan Thomas
'This Be the Verse'—Philip Larkin
'The Whitsun Weddings'—Philip Larkin
'Stop All the Clocks'—W. H. Auden (see page 55)
'Christmas'—John Betjeman

'Fern Hill'—Dylan Thomas
'Let Me Die a Youngman's Death'—Roger McGough
'The Subaltern's Love Song'—John Betjeman

Using the list above try the following activities:

◆ Members of the class seek out all the poems on the list, and groups present them in readers' theatre manner. Then the class votes on their choices, after trying to determine what made **'Warning'** so popular. Jenny Joseph, an English poet, wrote **'Warning'** about thirty years ago, when she was a young and harassed housewife. Seek out some of her other poems (she has published several volumes of verse) and compare them with her most popular poem.

◆ After completing their study of the poems in *Snapshots of Planet Earth*, members of the class vote on the most popular poems and then investigate the reading habits and tastes of the wider community. This would involve constructing a questionnaire and then trialling it with a small group (perhaps the teaching staff) to iron out ambiguities, etc. before polling relatives and friends.

◆ Every year there is a competition (The Archibald Prize) for portrait painters held in Sydney. The prize is awarded for the best portrait of a well-known person. Write a portrait description, i.e. paint a picture in words, of a person you have found interesting, or who you know very well. The following list might help you construct such a description: physical features (hair, dress, posture, poise, movement, general appearance); things he or she says, voice or sounds; behaviour/habits/specific interests, other things that make him/her special.

◆ Once you have written some details about your character of interest you can begin to recast what you have written by using metaphor.

A Note on Metaphor

A metaphor is a way of saying something in which a comparison is made between two objects by identifying one with the other. For instance, a comparison may be made by making a definite statement, as in:

> For on the sand the grey-wolf sea lies snarling
> (Judith Wright, **'The Surfer'**)

or, it may be inferred as in:

> Tiger, Tiger, burning bright
> In the forests of the night.
> (William Blake, **'Tiger, Tiger'**)

Metaphor is also used widely in everyday speech and often adds colour and vividness to expression. For instance in the media, sports commentators often indulge in metaphorical flourishes in order to bring their commentaries to life. For example:

'Slater has twinkle-toed footwork, is restless for runs, and fizzes at the crease like newly poured lemonade.'

Michael Flanagan, in an article entitled *At last, Carlton finds the power*, wrote: 'David Rhys-Jones was as agitated as a severed nerve when he took the field for yesterday's qualifying final between . . .'

'Justin Madden towered above his opponents like a crane derrick, dispensing the ball at will to the shoal of small, swift players who swept past him . . .'

'The second quarter was football at its best, . . . the ball rushing from one end of the ground to the other as if it were carrying messages between the goal umpires.'

An Activity on Clichés and Metaphoric Language

There is a difference between imaginative language and trite expressions. Here are some examples of poetic language and an accompanying trite expression. It is easy to have some fun by taking a well-known poem, in this case *The Rime of the Ancient Mariner* by Samuel Taylor Coleridge, and seeing what might be made of it in more colloquial terms:

Coleridge wrote:	We might say:
All in a hot and copper sky, The bloody Sun, at noon, . . .	a boiling sun
And every tongue, through utter drought, Was withered at the root, . . .	dying of thirst
Fear at my heart, as at a cup, My lifeblood seemed to sip!	scared to death

◆ Write down as many clichés as you can think of and then attempt to write a ballad stanza to illustrate one or two of them. (See the Ballads and Stories section for examples of the ballad form to use as models for your writing.)

◆ In groups, share your efforts to see if you can guess which cliché the ballad stanza was based on.

Landscapes and Still Life

The Winter Pond

The winter pond
Is as lonely as an old man's heart—
The heart that has tasted in full the sorrows in life.
The winter pond
Is as dry as an old man's eyes—
The eyes that have long lost their lustre through perpetual
    drudgery.

The winter pond
Is as desolate as an old man's hair—
The hair that is ash-white and sparse as frosted grass.
The winter pond
Is as despondent as a grief-stricken old man,
The old man bent beneath the downcast canopy of sky.

Ai' Ch'ing   *(translated by Julie C. Lin)*
[Chinese]

Winter Afternoon

A fruit bat skims along the lights.
The lakes's not calm, but fishermen
persist; a brown duck fights
through whipping reeds. And so again

it's time for the starlings to flock
and squabble for a place to perch.
The waves break on a small grey rock.

Scaling the scene by rule and clock;
there's reason, though why search
a reason for my symbols of stability?

The bat skims along the lights again.
Waves wear down a small grey rock.
Fishermen, rock, fragments, all contain
something more complex than reality.

Robert Adamson
[Australian]

Into the Landscape

The waste from the chemical factory's stacks
shivers on the wind
in the world above the shallow drain-fed lake.

Here where delight is a paddle-and-splash,
mothers can see
that the notice-board's warning
of danger-in-bathing
is wrong.

The mozaic of grits
on the dark wet bodies
surprises the eye
with its violet and brown

Coming in from the sea,
the sand looks beige,
and the lake-outlet merely a dribble.

Everything has been accepted
by the fifty fairy penguins
dead at the lick of the tide.

J. S. Harry
[Australian]

The Song of The Whale

Heaving mountain in the sea,
Whale, I heard you
Grieving.

Great whale, crying for your life,
Crying for your kind, I knew
How we would use
Your dying:

Lipstick for our painted faces,
Polish for our shoes.

Tumbling mountain in the sea,
Whale, I heard you
Calling.

Bird-high notes, keening, soaring:
At their edge a tiny drum
Like a heartbeat.

We would make you
Dumb.

In the forest of the sea,
Whale, I heard you
Singing,

Singing to your own kind.
We'll never let you be.
Instead of life we choose

Lipstick for our painted faces,
Polish for our shoes.

Kit Wright
[British]

Breakers

These lapdogs of the sea
Which lick the proffered hand
Turn savage suddenly,

Dig teeth into the sand,
Foam at the mouth and roar
As though they'd wreck the land.

And yet, being no more
Than water, they can't feel
Ashamed, or see the sore.

When by mere chance they steal
Our lovers, or inflict
A wound that will not heal:

They tear what they have licked;
Then suddenly make good—
Fawn on the derelict

Like pups that beg for food.

Edward Lowbury
[British]

Pine Tree

When the planners breached at last
the government plantation they left
a single sentry on our land,
a full-grown pine.

We hear its winter dialogue with
the wind: its gesturing branches cancel
neighbours, bring the snow-filled ranges
to our door.

Patient as a tethered horse
it stands in summer, as we drink
and watch our afternoons come loose
and drift away.

And so, inscrutable, it rides
with us across the shrinking seasons,
I contemplate the man who, forty
years ago,

on orders, first disturbed this soil
and set the seedling down, knowing
it would rise three feet in every
year he withered.

Geoff Page
[Australian]

Ash Wednesday

If the world is going to end
it will end
on a day like today
It's an end of the world day

If the world is going to end
it will end with cars
flinching through dust
headlights on in the heat

it will end in lifts
in buildings black from power failures
expecting a frayed spinning fall
any instant

If the world is going to end
it will end with fire
the haphazard destruction of fire
a wall of wind like a blowtorch

it will end with us inside the oven
inside smoke   inside explosions
fragments of us
a meltdown

If the world is going to end
it will end on a day like today
a pungent smell
and a thinning cloud of dead ash

Peter Macfarlane
[Australian]

The Meaning

Last night a pair of eyes
shone back at me
when I poked the torch out
the side door to see

what had made the dog
go off like a crude alarm,
echoing his urgency
across the still farm;

a pair of eyes
over near the chook shed,
low down, close together
and like Mars, faintly red.

Probably a neighbour's cat,
or a feral one,
its guts full of all
the damage it had done.

I told the dog to shut up
like you would a child
and went back to bed
where the doona was piled

roughly at the bottom
with the sheet,
a big sack of feathers
losing my body heat.

This morning at first light,
with a heavy frost
sheeting the ground.
I counted the cost

of my mistake—
our six chooks dead
and scattered in bits
in their corrugated shed.

It looked as if there'd been
a pillow fight
that got out of hand:
blood on the white

feathers, dead eyes open
and astonished, legs
bitten off, and the remains
of broken eggs.

I happened to look up
and saw a fox
running away through
the white far paddocks.

It ferreted across
the grass's frozen quilt
with enough speed
to resemble guilt,

a wriggling blip
on the monochrome
of a large computer screen.
Heading back home

it stopped once,
and turned and scanned
this farm, as if blood
were the meaning of the land.

Philip Hodgins
[*Australian*]

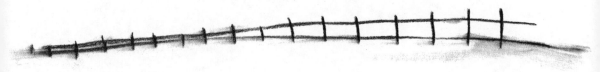

Notes

As pointed out in the note on readers' theatre in the introduction to *Snapshots of Planet Earth*, 'The Song of the Whale' by Englishman Kit Wright is very suitable for oral presentation. Wright has said that he was trying not only to make a protest about the slaughter of whales, but also, by his choice of words, to suggest the sound whales make—often referred to as their 'singing'.

'The Winter Pond' by the Chinese poet Ai' Ch'ing gains its effect by a succession of similes of desolate old age. The Australian poet Robert Adamson, who lives just north of Sydney, describes in 'Winter Afternoon' a winter landscape that is much less bleak.

Activities

Here are some opportunities for writing, and a suggestion for readers' theatre:

◆ Add some further similes of old age to 'The Winter Pond', or

◆ Describe in poetry or prose a winter landscape with which you are familiar.

◆ In your group, prepare a readers' theatre presentation of 'The Song of the Whale'. The Planet Earth Corp. has produced a CD entitled *Music and Songs from the Humpbacked Whales of Hervey Bay, Queensland*. You could use this recording as background to your readers' theatre presentation of Kit Wright's poem.

Love and Other Catastrophes

Love

Is it like a carnival with spangles and balloons,
Fancy-dress and comic masks and sun-drenched
    afternoons
Without a cloud to spoil the blue perfection of the
skies?
*'Well yes, at first, but later on it might seem
    otherwise.'*

Is it like a summer night when stock and roses
    stain
The silken dark with fragrance and the nightingale
    again
Sweetly pierces silence with its silver blades of
    song?
*'I say once more it can be thus, but not for very
    long.'*

Is it like a great parade with drums and marching
    feet
And everybody cheering them, and dancing in the
    street,
With laughter swirling all around and only tears of
    joy?
*'If that alone, you'd find the fun would soon begin to
    cloy.'*

Is it like the falling snow, noiseless through the
    night;
Mysterious as moonlight and innocent and bright,
Changing the familiar world with its hypnotic spell?
*'It has been known to be like that, and other things
    as well.*

'But if you find, when all the brightest ribbons have
    grown frayed,
The colours faded, music dumb, and all that great parade
Dismissed into the darkness where the moon has
    been put out,
Together you find warmth and strength, then that's
    what it's about.'

Vernon Scannell
[British]

I will give my love an apple without e'er a core

I will give my love an apple without e'er a core,
I will give my love a house without e'er a door,
I will give my love a palace wherein she may be
And she may unlock it without e'er a key.

My head is the apple without e'er a core,
My mind is the house without e'er a door,
My heart is the palace wherein she may be
And she may unlock it without e'er a key.

Anon.

Prize-Giving

Professor Eisenbart, asked to attend
a girls' school speech night as an honoured guest
and give the prizes out, rudely declined;
but from indifference agreed, when pressed
with dry scholastic jokes, to change his mind,
to grace their humble platform, and to lend

distinction (of a kind not specified)
to the occasion. Academic dress
became him, as he knew. When he appeared
the girls whirred with an insect nervousness,
the Head in humbler black flapped round and steered
her guest, superb in silk and fur, with pride

to the best seat beneath half-hearted blooms
tortured to form the school's elaborate crest.
Eisenbart scowled with violent distaste,
then recomposed his features to their best
advantage: deep in thought, with one hand placed
like Rodin's Thinker. So he watched the room's

mosaic of young heads. Blonde, black, mouse-brown
they bent for their Headmistress' opening prayer.
But underneath a light (no accident
of seating, he felt sure), with titian hair
one girl sat grinning at him, her hand bent
under her chin in mockery of his own.

Speeches were made and prizes given. He shook
indifferently a host of virgin hands.
"*Music*!" The girl with titian hair stood up,
hitched at a stocking, winked at nearby friends,
and stood before him to receive a cup
of silver chased with curious harps. He took

her hand, and felt its voltage fling his hold
from his calm age and power; suffered her strange
eyes, against reason dark, to take his stare
with her to the piano, there to change
her casual schoolgirl's for a master's air.
He forged his rose-hot dream as Mozart told

the fullness of all passion or despair
summoned by arrogant hands. The music ended,
Eisenbart teased his gown while others clapped,
and peered into a trophy which suspended
his image upside down: a sage fool trapped
by music in a copper net of hair.

Gwen Harwood
[Australian]

The Pop Star's Song

O how I love you baby,
O baby you're just swell;
I love your eyes, they're magic;
You've got me in your spell.

I love you in the summer,
But baby I'll be there
When autumn leaves have shrivelled
And winter chills the air.

I'm crazy for you baby;
All the day and night
I dream of you in colour
As well as black-and-white.

O baby you're the music
Of heavenly guitars;
Your skin is soft as moonlight,
Your eyes shine like the stars.

I love you madly baby;
You know I really do.
I think you know the reason—
I'm a baby too!

I'm a drooling baby,
And you don't mind a bit;
I yowl and howl in public
And I get paid for it!

So baby let's get married
And one day there might be
With luck another baby
As fortunate as me.

Vernon Scannell
[British]

Scaffolding

Masons, when they start upon a building,
Are careful to test out the scaffolding;

Make sure the planks won't slip at busy points,
Secure all ladders, tighten bolted joints.

And yet all this comes down when the job's done
Showing off walls of sure and solid stone.

So if, my dear, there sometimes seem to be
Old bridges breaking between you and me

Never fear. We may let the scaffolds fall
Confident that we have built our wall.

Seamus Heaney
[Irish]

It's Raining in Love

I don't know what it is,
but I distrust myself
when I start to like a girl
    a lot.

It makes me nervous
I don't say the right things
or perhaps I start
    to examine,
             evaluate
                  compute
    what I am saying.

If I say, "Do you think it's going to rain?"
and she says, "I don't know,"
I start thinking; Does she really like me?

In other words
I get a little creepy.

A friend of mine once said,
"It's twenty times better to be friends
    with someone
than it is to be in love with them."

I think he's right and besides,
it's raining somewhere, programming flowers
and keeping snails happy
    That's all taken care of.

BUT
if a girl likes me a lot
and starts getting real nervous
and suddenly begins asking me funny questions
and looks sad if I give the wrong answers
and she says things like,
"Do you think it's going to rain?
and I say, "It beats me,"
and she says, "Oh,"
and looks a little sad
at the clear blue California sky,
I think: Thank God, it's you, baby, this time
    instead of me.

Richard Brautigan
[USA]

Symptoms

Although you have given me a stomach upset,
weak knees, a lurching heart, a fuzzy brain,
a high-pitched laugh, a monumental phone bill,
a feeling of unworthiness, sharp pain
when you are somewhere else, a guilty conscience,
a longing, and a dread of what's in store,
a pulse rate for the *Guinness Book of Records* —
life now is better than it was before.

Although you have given me a raging temper,
insomnia, a rising sense of panic,
a hopeless challenge, bouts of introspection,
raw, bitten nails, a voice that's strangely manic,
a selfish streak, a fear of isolation,
a silly smile, lips that are chapped and sore,
a running joke, a risk, an inspiration —
life now is better than it was before.

Although you have given me a premonition,
chattering teeth, a goal, a lot to lose,
a granted wish, mixed motives, superstitions,
hang-ups and headaches, fear of awful news,
a bubble in my throat, a dare to swallow,
a crack of light under a closing door,
the crude, fantastic prospect of forever —
life now is better than it was before.

Sophie Hannah
[British]

Stop All the Clocks

Stop all the clocks, cut off the telephone,
Prevent the dog from barking with a juicy bone,
Silence the pianos and with muffled drum
Bring out the coffin, let the mourners come.

Let aeroplanes circle moaning overhead
Scribbling on the sky the message He Is Dead,
Put crêpe bows round the white necks of the public doves,
Let the traffic policemen wear black cotton gloves.

He was my North, my South, my East and West,
My working week and my Sunday rest,
My noon, my midnight, my talk, my song;
I thought that love would last for ever: I was wrong.

The stars are not wanted now: put out every one;
Pack up the moon and dismantle the sun;
Pour away the ocean and sweep up the wood.
For nothing now can ever come to any good.

W. H. Auden
[British]

Love's Coming

Quietly as rosebuds
    Talk to the thin air,
Love came so lightly
    I knew not he was there.

Quietly as lovers
    Creep at the middle moon,
Softly as players tremble
    In the tears of a tune;

Quietly as lilies
    Their faint vows declare
Came the shy pilgrim:
    I knew not he was there

Quietly as tears fall
    On a wild sin,
Softly as grief's call
    In a violin;

Without hail or tempest,
    Blue sword or flame,
Love came so lightly
    I knew not that he came.

John Shaw Neilson
[Australian]

A Day Too Late

You meet a man. You're looking for a hero,
Which you pretend he is. A day too late
You realise his sex appeal is zero
And you begin to dread the second date.

You'd love to stand him up but he's too clever —
He knows by heart your work and home address.
Last night he said he'd stay with you forever.
You fear he might have meant it. What a mess!

That's when you start regretting his existence.
It's all his fault. You hate him with a passion.
You hate his love, his kindness, his persistence.
He's too intense. His clothes are out of fashion.

Shortly you reach the stage of desperation.
At first you thought about behaving well
And giving him an honest explanation.
Now all you want to say is 'Go to Hell',

And even that seems just a touch too gentle.
Deep down, the thing that makes you want to weep
Is knowing that you once felt sentimental
About this wholly unattractive creep.

Sophie Hannah
[British]

Passengers to the City

This morning she is travelling
eyes steeled on her knitting,
while the man next to her
from time to time turns his head,
glances briefly at the fiery wool
then look away.

He is silent as a guard, and she
never speaks. Are they together, some pair
perfectly joined by silence?
Or are they today's complete strangers?

I'll never know, left simply
to knit them together — characters in a story,
a middle-aged couple on a train
waiting for love's fable to happen
to them, for their old lives to be
swept aside, changed, changed —
as she keeps knitting, bumping him
occasionally, at which he shrugs,
turns his head quickly
not like a lover, but content.

Katherine Gallagher
[Australian]

Suburban Lovers

Every morning they hold hands
on the fleet diesel that interprets them
like music on a roller-piano as they move
over the rhythmic rails. Her thoughts lie
kitten-curled in his while the slats of living
racket past them, back yards greying
with knowledge, embankments blazoned
with pig-face whose hardihood
be theirs, mantling with pugnacious flowers
stratas of clay, blank sandstone, sustaining them
against year's seepage, rain's intolerance.

Each evening they cross the line
while the boom-gate's slender arms constrain
the lines of waiting cars.
Stars now have flown up out of the east.
They halt at her gate. Next-door's children
scatter past, laughing. They smile. The moon,
calm as a seashore, raises its pale face.
Their hands dance in the breeze blowing
from a hundred perfumed gardens. On the cliff of kissing
they know this stillness come down upon them like a cone.
All day it has been suspended there, above their heads.

Bruce Dawe
[Australian]

Dinner at My Sister's

Throughout those meals the slaughtering went on.
Like the blind French aristocracy who ate
With wolfish indifference at Trianon
While the mob howled bloody murder at the gate,
We'd sit there over our heaped platefuls. George,
My brother-in-law, reeking from the styes,
Forked down the hot food, grunted fierce replies
To a son who read land-sales from the *Gazette*
As though they were some spiritual exercise.
My sister sat, or served; the Tilly lamp
Flared like a torch in a vestibule of Hell.
On either side of the lamp, on looking up,
One saw the drear slow-motion agonies,
On viscous fly-papers, of captive flies.
The family scorned with ease their suffragette

Stick-at-it-iveness, the stir of legs and wings
Seemed emblem of all bondage only to me
—Two species in conflict, tottering
Each through its own *Totentanz*, tediously
Kicking against the fatal honeyed measure.
So, too, George wolfed away, until such time
As he himself confronted on his plate
A struggling wretch whose throes apostrophized
Such appetites, whose individual buzz
Sickened with its persistence, more than when
It pleaded with its brothers common cause
As they twirled in murmuring ribbons overhead.

Bruce Dawe
[Australian]

Unholy Marriage

POLICE ARE SEEKING TO IDENTIFY THE PILLION
RIDER WHO WAS ALSO KILLED

Her mother bore her, father cared
And clothed her body, young and neat.
The careful virgin had not shared
Cool soft anointment of her breast
Or any other sweet,
But kept herself for best.

How sweet she would have been in bed,
Her bridegroom sighing in her hair,
His tenderness heaped on her head,
Receiving benediction from her breast
With every other fair
She kept for him, the best.

Who she is now they do not know
Assembling her body on a sheet.
This foolish virgin shared a blow
That drove her almost through a stranger's breast
And all her sweet
Mingles with his in dust.

Unwilling marriage, her blood runs with one
Who bought for a few pounds and pence
A steel machine able to 'do a ton',
Not knowing at a ton a straw will pierce a breast:
No wheel has built-in sense,
Not yet the shiniest and best.

And so, 'doing a ton', in fog and night
Before he could think, Christ! or she could moan
There came a heavy tail without a light
And many tons compressed each back to breast
And blood and brain and bone
Mixed, lay undressed.

Anointed only by the punctured oil
Poured like unleashed wind or fire from bag
Sold by some damned magician out to spoil
The life that girded in this young girl's breast
Now never to unfurl her flag
And march love's happy quest.

Her mother hears the clock: her father sighs,
Takes off his boots: she's late tonight,
I hope she's a careful virgin: men have eyes
For cherished daughters growing in the breast.
Some news? They hear the gate
A man comes: not the best.

David Holbrook
[British]

The passionate Sheepheard to his love

Come live with mee, and be my love,
And we will all the pleasures prove,
That Vallies, groves, hills and fieldes,
Woods, or steepie mountaine yeeldes.

And wee will sit upon the Rocks,
Seeing the Sheepheards feede theyr flocks,
By shallow Rivers, to whose falls
Melodious byrds sing Madrigalls.

And I will make these beds of Roses,
And a thousand fragrant posies,
A cap of flowers, and a kirtle,
Imbroydred all with leaves of Mirtle.

A gowne made of the finest wooll.
Which from our pretty Lambes we pull,
Fayre lined slippers for the cold:
With buckles of the purest gold.

A belt of straw, and Ivie buds,
With Corall clasps and Amber studs,
And if these pleasures may thee move,
Come live with mee, and by my love.

The Sheepheards Swaines shall daunce and sing,
For thy delight each May-morning.
If these delights thy minde may move,
Then live with mee, and be my love.

Christopher Marlowe
[English]

The Nimphs reply to the Sheepheard

If all the world and love were young,
And truth in every Sheepheards tongue,
These pretty pleasures might me move,
To live with thee, and be thy love.

Time drives the flocks from field to fold,
When Rivers rage, and Rocks grow cold,
And *Philomell* becommeth dombe,
The rest complaines of cares to come,

The flowers doe fade, and wanton fieldes,
To wayward winter reckoning yeeldes;
A honny tongue, a hart of gall,
Is fancies spring, but sorrowes fall.

Thy gownes, thy shooes, thy beds of Roses,
Thy cap, thy kirtle, and thy posies,
Soone breake, soone wither, soone forgotten:
In follie ripe, in reason rotten.

Thy belt of straw and Ivie buddes,
Thy Corall claspes and Amber studdes,
All these in mee no meanes can move,
To come to thee, and be thy love.

But could youth last, and love still breede,
Had joyes no date, nor age no neede,
Then these delights my minde might move,
To live with thee, and be thy love.

Sir Walter Raleigh
[English]

Come Live With Me and be My Girl

If you'll give me a kiss and be my girl
Jump on my bike, we'll do a ton.
We'll explode from the city in a cloud of dust
And roar due west to the setting sun.

We'll bounce the day all over the beach
Pop them like seaweed and scatter ourselves
Careless as kids with candy floss
Into all the shapes of all the shells.

We'll go as giddy as merry-go-rounds,
Bump with a crash like dodgem cars,
Float in a basket of coloured balloons
Or jump in a rocket and whizz for Mars.

If you love to be blown by a roar of wind,
If you love to twist and spin and twirl,
If you love to crash on the shore like waves,
Then give me a kiss and be my girl.

I love to be blown by a roar of wind,
But I love to watch the sea asleep,
And breathe in salt and fresh-caught shrimps
As we wind our way through snoring streets.

I'll jive in a cellar till the band drops dead
But I want you to sing on your own guitar
For no one but me and a moonlight oak
Then dive in the silent lake for a star.

I love to twist the night away
But I love to hold you dark and still.
I love your kick that drives us miles
But I love the view from the top of the hill.

But if you give me the crashing waves
And sing me the blues of the sea as well,
Then, whether there's candyfloss or not,
I'll give you a kiss and be your girl.

Leo Aylen
[British]

Notes

Modern pop lyrics make a useful comparison with the anonymously written **'I will give my love an apple'**, which is about two centuries old. Few song lyrics are more beautiful than this.

'Prize-Giving'

Rodin's Thinker—a famous sculpture of a person sitting with chin resting on a hand. The image is now so well known in Western culture that it has been widely used to represent a person thinking

mosaic—an arrangement of small pieces of different coloured stone, tile, glass, etc., inlaid to form a picture or design on a pavement or a wall

titian hair—reddish brown coloured hair (a reference to the painter Titian, who often painted women with hair of that colour)

forged—The poet simultaneously draws on at least two meanings of this word: the use of heat and hammer form or mould, as well as the notion of slowly moving something ahead.

Born in Brisbane, Gwen Harwood (1920–1995) moved to Tasmania in 1945 where she lived for the rest of her life. She began to write poetry in her late thirties in 'an attempt', as she once said, 'to realise in words the moments that gave my life its meaning'.

'Symptoms'

bouts of introspection—examinations of an individual's own mental states or processes; looking into oneself

Sophie Hannah (born 1971 in Manchester) is a skilful practitioner of light verse. Her work and that of her compatriot Wendy Cope are strongly recommended to students wishing to pursue their own poetry reading. **'Symptoms'** pairs well with Vernon Scannell's **'Love'**. There are two other poems by Sophie Hannah in this collection: **'A Day Too Late'** (page 56) and **'Summary of a Western'** (page 117).

'Scaffolding'

Seamus Heaney, the Irish poet and Nobel Prize winner, has in **'Scaffolding'** written a simple poem in rhyming couplets, another form that students might like to imitate. Note, however, that, in contrast, say, to Alexander Pope's rhyming couplets, the metre is somewhat irregular, bringing it closer to everyday speech.

'Stop All the Clocks'

These lines have recently become very popular through being featured in the film *Four Weddings and a Funeral*. They first appeared in Auden and Isherwood's play *The Ascent of F6* but were then partially rewritten as one of *Four Cabaret Songs for Miss Hedli Anderson*. In *The Ascent of F6* the first two stanzas are as printed on page 55, but then the poem continues:

Hold up your umbrellas to keep off the rain
From Doctor Williams while he opens a vein;
Life, he pronounces, it is finally extinct.
Sergeant, arrest that man who said he winked!

There are two more stanzas, referring to characters in the play:

Shawcross will say a few words sad and kind
To the weeping crowds about the Master-Mind,
While Lamp with a powerful microscope
Searches their faces for a sign of hope.

And Gunn, of course, will drive the motor-hearse:
None could drive it better, most would drive it worse.
He'll open up the throttle to its fullest power
And drive him to the grave at ninety miles an hour.

◆ Consider, after making due allowance for the references to the play included here, whether you detect any differences in tone.

'Love's Coming'
John Shaw Neilson (1872–1942) was perhaps Australia's best lyric poet before the Second World War. He had less than three years' schooling, and until 1928 was an itinerant labourer, working on the roads and on farms. **'Love's Coming'** was first published in 1911; his most famous poem is the mystical **'The Orange Tree'**.

'A Day Too Late'
This poem would pair well with a poem by Wendy Cope, 'Love Story', the eighth poem in her sequence 'From June to December', in her collection *Making Cocoa for Kingsley Amis* (Faber & Faber, 1986). This and Sophie Hannah's *The Hero and the Girl Next Door* (Carcanet, 1995) are essential for all school libraries, as both poets appeal strongly to older adolescents.

'Passengers to the City'
Katherine Gallagher (b. 1935) is an Australian writer who lives in Victoria. This poem brings into the open such speculations of travellers on public transport as what are the other people who are sharing the carriage like; are they together; what is the relationship between them? It also captures the awkwardness of two people seated together on public transport each of them somewhat embarrassed about invading the other's personal space.

'Suburban Lovers'
roller-piano—a mechanical device driven by air pressure which caused the hammers of the piano to strike the strings. Piano rolls were made from sturdy paper with holes punched in the appropriate places to set off the hammers. The person 'playing' the piano roll was required to pump the bellows with his/her feet,

no piano keys were played. The Roller-pianos were popular fifty years ago in Australia and many households had one for home entertainment.

blazoned—brightly displayed

pig-face—a small ground-cover succulent with very brightly coloured flowers

'Suburban Lovers' and **'Dinner at My Sister's'** can be read individually and as a pair. Both poems are rich in imagery which evokes the suburban worlds of the lovers and a family dinner.

'Dinner at My Sister's'
Trianon—the favourite residence of Marie Antoinette, erected as a retreat by Louis XIV in the French town of Versailles. Living within the confines of the residence and the extensive English-style gardens, Marie Antoinette and the ladies of her court dressed up and pretended that they were peasants living a rustic lifestyle. While the aristocracy indulged themselves, the real peasants beyond the garden gates suffered poverty and starvation.

Tilly Lamp—a portable light which generated light from a mantle made from finely woven silk. The lamp was fuelled by kerosene.

Totentanz—a German word which refers to the Dance of Death—an artistic representation of the ever-present and universal power of death. In French, it is known as *la danse macabre*.

Bruce Dawe (b. 1930) is one of Australia's best known contemporary poets. He has published a number of volumes of poetry, written with energy and humour about Australian life. He has had a variety of manual jobs and spent nine years in the RAAF. He now works at the University of Southern Queensland.

'The passionate Sheepheard' and 'The Nimphs reply'
In 1599 Christopher Marlowe published his love poem, **'The passionate Sheepheard to his love'**. In the following year Sir Walter Ralegh/Raleigh answered him with **'The Nimphs reply to the Sheepheard'**, using the same style and form.

Activities

◆ You will have noticed that Vernon Scannell's **'Love'** is constructed in question and answer form. See if you can construct your own poem imitating the question-and-answer pattern.

◆ One of the Mersey poets (writers from the city of Liverpool on the Mersey River in England) Adrian Henri has written a poem, **'Love Is . . .'**, which is not included here. The form lends itself to easy imitation, so we offer one stanza from it. (The whole poem is included in Roger McGough's anthology *Strictly Private* (Penguin) and in the collection *Penguin Poets No. 10*.)

> Love is the presents in Christmas shops
> Love is when you're feeling Top of the Pops
> Love is what happens when the music stops

◆ **'The Pop Star's Song'** lightly parodies the lyrics of pop music and the often colourful behaviour of pop musicians. Bring in the lyrics of your favourite pop songs for comparison with the Scannell poem. Is **'The Pop Star's Song'** simply a collection of the clichés to be found in pop songs from a particular era? List some of the clichés in current popular songs. What is the most popular song being played on your favourite radio station at present? What are the lyrics of this song about?

◆ Try writing out **'It's Raining in Love'** in continuous prose and then decide what, if anything, has been lost in the process.

◆ Using the scenario from Gallagher's poem, develop an improvisation which includes the poet's speculations about the other characters. Set up the scenario to allow the poet 'to speak her thoughts' to the audience, perhaps in a speech bubble in a cartoon, or an aside directed to the audience.

'I will give my love an apple'
◆ These are the first two stanzas of a much larger poem with an interesting structure. The first stanza provides a series of metaphors, each of which is explained in the second stanza. Use this structural device to try to write a poem of your own.

◆ Just as Raleigh replied to Marlowe, write a reply to Aylen's poem.

◆ The two Elizabethan poems have been printed with the original spellings in order that teachers may briefly explore the standardisation of English spelling that took place in the seventeenth and early eighteenth centuries, and the more recent attempts at spelling reform. David Crystal's *The Cambridge Encyclopedia of the English Language* is an excellent reference here.

School and Other Disasters

Around the High School

Listen
or not;
you'll hear
them anyway:
the thumping
bass and
rhythmic
drums
of cars
with men
and boys
in them,
their stereos
turned high,
all circling
the campus
like sleek
vultures
or loud
lions,
blasting out
to each of us
the macho
male's hard
dominance
and lewd
electric
mating
cries.

John Laue
[USA]

The Play Way

Sunlight pillars through glass, probes each desk
For milk tops, drinking straws and old dry crusts.
The music strides to challenge it
Mixing memory and desire with chalk dust.

My lesson notes read: Teacher will play
Beethoven's Concerto Number Five
And class will express themselves freely
In writing. One said 'Can we jive?'

When I produced the record, but now
The big sound has silenced them. Higher
And firmer, each authoritative note
Pumps the classroom up tight as a tyre

Working its private spell behind eyes
That stare wide. They have forgotten me
For once. The pens are busy, the tongues mime
Their blundering embrace of the free

Word. A silence charged with sweetness
Breaks short on lost faces where I see
New looks. Then notes stretch taut as snares. They trip
To fall into themselves unknowingly.

Seamus Heaney
[Irish]

Novel Lesson

Beneath the trees
Friday afternoon
that heat-wave week
in early February
the class on pine benches;
moss rocks
with a class-set novel
hurriedly borrowed
from the bookroom
because the hot school room
had turned us out
where pens slipped
in sweat-wet fingers.
But it happens sometimes,
where for an hour
the only noises
are flies and turning pages.

Quiet circles the class.
Each chapter
buries them deeper
in a fiction of the mind.
I hesitate to ask them
to finish the book
for weekend homework.
The siren beats me.
No one stirs to go.

They are not here.

Jeff Guess
[Australian]

What's in a Locker?

tennis shoe,
skateboard (blue),
book report—
overdue;
jacket (red),
cockroach (dead),
sandwich bag,
(week-old bread);
paper—lined.
grade slip—signed.
Oreo.
orange rind,
shorts (outgrown),
saxophone,
bubble gum
Choose your Own
Adventure (old),
sweatband (gold),
styling mousse—
(super hold);
Twinkie (looks
mouldy), hooks—
everything!
(except books!)

Fran Haraway
[USA]

To Let Her Think Shadows

I
This girl
this growing-up
fourteen-year-old
watches for eyes
watching
listens for words
admiring
aches
for something that
no teacher
no Hell he's old
and doesn't know
where we're up to
adult out-of-
their-world can
interpret. There
look
at her she
sits
head lowered
away from the pettiness
the what-in-the blazes-is
he-talking-about
dryness of my
pontification. Call
her up Well Marj
when are you going
to grow up and do
some work?
Words
words words growing
up is what
she's trying to
working at
dying to do.

II
Outside just
a window away
the sun the
seeping-into
sun the live the
lively (dust twitches
nostrils in
this drab room desks
defy the itch
in the limbs to
stretch) sun
out there saying
saying all
songs of things
like come
come
come yet Yes Sir
here she
sits
sitting reading
dull
words Land
Of Heart's Desire
or something
someone wrote
before that sun
came out
Wonders
what it's all
about but the sun
is shining
too outside to
let her
think
shadows.

B. A. Breen
[Australian]

The Spelling Prize

Every Child's Book of Animal Stories.
To compete, we stood on the wooden forms
that seated four in discomfort.
When you missed your word, you sat down
and wrote it out twenty times.
At last only two were left:
Ella and I, who had sailed
past *ghost, nymph, scheme, flight, nephew,*
the shoals of o - u - g - h
and i before e, stood waiting
for the final word, Whoever
put her hand up first when Sir
announced it, could try to spell it.
A pause, while Sir went outside.
Some of the girls started hissing,
"Give Ella a chance. Let her win."

Through the window I saw the playground
bare as a fowlyard, the ditch
in a paddock beyond where frogs
lived out whatever their life was
before the big boys impaled them
on wooden skewers, a glint
from a roof in the middle distance
that was Ella's home. I had been there

the week before, when my grandmother went
to take their baby, the ninth,
my brother's old shawl. Ella coaxed me
to a ramshackle tinroofed shed
where her father was killing a bull calf.
A velvety fan of blood
opened out on the concrete floor
as one of her brothers pumped the forelegs:
"You do this to empty the heart."

The father severed the head, and set it
aside on a bench where the eyes, still trusting,
looked back at what had become
of the world. It was not the sight
of the entrails, the deepening crimson
of blood that sent me crying
across the yard, but the calf's eyes watching
knife, whetstone, carcase, the hand that fed.

Ella followed. "I'll show you my toys."
In that house where nobody owned
a corner, a space they might call their own,
she kept two old dolls in a shoebox.
Below me the whispers continued:
"Let Ella win the prize."
Why, now, does memory brood
on Sir's return, and the moment

when he put down his cane and smoothed
his hair grease-tight on his skull
and snapped out the last word: MYSTIC,

a word never found in our Readers.
My innocent hand flew up.
Sheer reflex, but still, I knew it,
and knew I could slip in a k
or an i for a y and lose,

but did not, and sixty years
can't change it; I stand in the playground
and the pale dust stirs as my friends
of the hour before yell "Skite!"
and "Showoff!" and "Think you're clever".
They gather round Ella, who turns
one hurt look from her red-rimmed eyes
at my coveted, worthless prize.

Gwen Harwood
[Australian]

Examiner

The routine trickery of the examination
Baffles these hot and discouraged youths.
Driven by they know not what external pressure.
They pour their hated self-analysis
Through the nib of confession, onto the accusatory page.

I, who have plotted their immediate downfall.
I am entrusted with the divine categories,
ABCD and the hell of E,
The parade of prize and the backdoor of pass.

In the tight silence
Standing by a green grass window
Watching the fertile earth graduate its sons
With more compassion—not commanding the shape
Of stem and stamen, bringing the trees to pass
By shift of sunlight and increase of rain.
For each seed the whole soil, for the inner life
The environment receptive and contributory—
I shudder at the narrow frames of our text-book schools
In which we plant our so various seedlings.
Each brick-walled barracks
Cut into numbered rooms, black-boarded,
Ties the venturing shoot to the master's stick;
The screw-desk rows of lads and girls
Subdued in the shade of an adult—
Their acid subsoil—
Shape the new to the old in the ashen garden.

F. R. Scott
[British]

The Examination

(written at the Arvon Foundation, Totleigh Barton, Devon)

'Well doctor, what do you think?'
He took the poem and examined it.
'*Mmmm ...*'
The clock ticked nervously.
'*This will have to come out for a start.*'
He stabbed a cold finger into its heart.
'*Needs cutting here as well.*
This can go.
And this is weak. Needs building up.'
He paused ...
'*But it's the Caesura I'm afraid,*
Can't do much about that.'
My palms sweated.
'*Throw it away and start again, that's my advice.*
And on the way out, send in the next patient, will you?'

I buttoned up my manuscript and left.
Outside, it was raining odes and stanzas.
I caught a crowded anthology and went directly home.

Realizing finally that I would never be published.
That I was to remain one of the alltime great
      unknown poets,
My work rejected by even the vanity presses,
I decided to end it all.

Taking an overdose of Lyricism
I awaited the final peace
When into the room burst the Verse Squad
Followed by the Poetry Police.

Roger McGough
[British]

Whatever's the matter with Melanie?

Whatever's the matter with Melanie?
They say her Dad's run off and that's bad luck,
but no excuse for treating friends like muck.

Whatever's the matter with Melanie?
She never talked about her Dad before,
but says she hates him now. I'm not so sure
she even knows her own mind any more.

Whatever's the matter with Melanie?
She has no cause to take things out on me
who was the first to tell her how her Dad
went queer the day he lost his job, how we
found him staring in the lift, his eyes gone dead.

Whatever's the matter with Melanie?
I only called her 'Melon' once and pulled
her hair a bit to show I didn't hold
a grudge against her for the change. She whirled
like a top. I've never seen her eyes so cold.

I couldn't stop a laugh — she looked so queer.
That glassy look! 'You're just the same,' I cried,
'as your old man when he was on the beer.'
I told the truth and never would have lied,
whatever's the matter with Melanie.

It makes no difference now. She hit my nose
with fists like flint, sent exploding light
jagging through my head. Now her true self shows:
that's no way for a normal girl to fight,
whatever's the matter with Melanie.

Mum told me people judge me by my friends
and I'm glad I'm one who understands
how people feel. So this is where our friendship ends,
whatever's the matter with Melanie.

I shan't forgive Miss Law who sat and talked with her
and held her hand — not mine — and that's not fair,
whatever's the matter with Melanie.

Barrie Wade
[British]

The Green Rambler

It had no radio
And a three-speed shift on the column.
The dent in front I had made
Slamming into the wall of the Rialto.

Nancy and I, after steaming the windows,
Were driving in sleet late for home.
The curve was long and gentle,
But the ice thick and falling.

When I lost control,
The car spun like a leaf,
Swirled us backward into a fence,
Tore up yards of barbed wire.

Time sagged, became time enough
To weep, curse, regret, and wrestle
My craning date to the floor, fearing
The car would be sliced like cheese.

But we survived, Nancy and I
And the green Rambler, stripped of trim,
Minus a handle, but alive,
There in the icy field.

Home was the hard part.
Dad in the kitchen in the same chair
As when I left, I had told him
I was going nowhere but school.

He lit a cigarette.
I confessed the whole thing,
Nancy, the car, the barbed wire.
I'll pay, I said.

He went out, ran his hands
Over the car's wounds. Grounded for sure
I thought. But all he said was,
Could have been worse.

Much worse, I knew.
And suddenly knew that he knew. The whole thing.
Even before I left.

And that knowing,
like a friendly scar,
I still carry.

Dennis DePauw
[USA]

Mid-term Break

I sat all morning in the college sick bay
Counting bell knelling classes to a close.
At two o'clock our neighbours drove me home.

In the porch I met my father crying—
He had always taken funerals in his stride—
And Big Jim Evans saying it was a hard blow.

The baby cooed and laughed and rocked the pram
When I came in, and I was embarrassed
By old men standing up to shake my hand

And tell me they were 'sorry for my trouble.'
Whispers informed strangers I was the eldest,
Away at school, as my mother held my hand

In hers and coughed out angry tearless sighs.
At ten o'clock the ambulance arrived
With the corpse, stanched and bandaged by the nurses.

Next morning I went up into the room. Snowdrops
And candles soothed the bedside; I saw him
For the first time in six weeks. Paler now,

Wearing a poppy bruise on his left temple,
He lay in the four foot box as in his cot.
No gaudy scars, the bumper knocked him clear.

A four foot box, a foot for every year.

Seamus Heaney
[Irish]

# Notes

This selection of poems offers diverse perspectives on school experiences by contemporary Australian poets (Jeff Guess and B. A. Breen), North American poets (John Laue and Fran Haraway), the English poets Barrie Wade and Roger McGough, and the Nobel laureate Seamus Heaney. (See also the Love and Other Catastrophes section).

'The Play Way'
This poem by Seamus Heaney, takes its title from Caldwell Cook's influential book on English teaching *The Play Way*, which advocated the involvement of students in intense, absorbing activity as the best means of achieving competence in English. The poem could be compared with D. H. Lawrence's 'The Best of School'. For the adventurous, Lawrence's 'Last Lesson of the Afternoon' provides a sharp contrast.

'To Let Her Think Shadows'
This poem uses at least three voices: the young girl's voice, the voice of the teacher, and that of the poet. The poem should be read aloud, paying particular attention to these different voices and to the corresponding shifts in mood. You will need time to read the poem several times and to note the change of voices. This poem would be interesting for a readers' theatre performance.

The poems by Gwen Harwood and F. R. Scott extend the theme of school but evoke two sharply defined moments in time. In each poem complex and ambivalent emotions are recalled as the protagonist, the child in **'The Spelling Prize'**; and the teacher in **'Examiner'** contemplate an action of compromise and conflict. In **'Examiner'** students often misread the teacher's stance as presented in the first two stanzas, seeing it as colluding with the savage world of the examination. Take time to discover how the sustained metaphor of the blighted seedling that holds the second half of the poem together reveals the teacher's despair at the conflicting roles of nurturer and examiner.

Try writing a piece similar to Roger McGough's witty poem **'The Examination'**.

vanity press—This term, more often referred to as vanity publishing, refers to writers who, having failed to find a publisher, finance their own publications.

Activities

◆ **'What's in a Locker?'** provides an ideal model for writing. Try writing your own answer to the question, following the same structure. A variation might be: What's in a School Bag/Backpack?

◆ In **'Examiner'**, how does the teacher feel while standing by the window supervising the examination? Talk this over in your group.

◆ There are numerous collections of poems about school in other anthologies. In your group, make a collection of school poems.

◆ **'Whatever's the matter with Melanie?'** provides an interesting example of an unreliable narrator. Discuss what is it about this poem that makes you want to side with Melanie rather than with the narrator?

Playing with Language

Not Enough Dough? Tough!

A poem written after reading a Dictionary of English Pronunciation.

You are advised to recite the poem aloud, taking care to make each line rhyme exactly with the one above it.

Toast her, all, in parsnip wine,
This poem's pleasant heroine!
Whose father oft dipped in his wallet
To buy her tickets for the ballet
Of all his girls he loved her most —
That's why he didn't count the cost.
All day he toiled, at tedious work,
T'afford her favourite dish ('twas pork).
And tirelessly the good man strove
To give her luxury — and love!
It was in honour of his Mary
That he pursued a high salary.
The very soaps she used to wash
Required a great expense of cash —
But as he once said to her aunt
(A lady elderly and gaunt):
'The purchase of the best hair-drier
I'd not consider cavalier
If it would mean my Mary'd have
No worries with her permanent wave!
(He, incidentally, was clever,
The inventor of little lever.
Which Hi-fi fanciers attach —

When they are playing Brahms or Bach —
To the treasured gramophone:
An operation eas'ly done!)
In winter he would call her: 'Hi!
My dear, go off at once and ski
In Switzerland. And don't forget
To buy yourself a new beret!'
In the garden with his mower
He'd stop to gather her a flower.
(What an action — so to gather
Flowers for Mary! — splendid father!)
Himself invariably as spruce
As some newly grown lettuce,
He nibbled, every day at one,
Some sandwich, or a simple scone.
'The money saved,' he often said,
'Shall at my Mary's feet be laid.'

Alas — I hate to use the word —
The day came when 'I can't afford
It, Mary,' he was forced to howl.
She was feeding from a bowl
(Which somehow seemed to make it worse)
Her much-loved Alf — a well-groomed horse.
The time had come, he said, to warn
Her that she'd have to learn to darn
Her stockings, and would have by half
To cut the hay she fed to Alf.
'I fear,' he cried, 'from this day forth
My stocks and shares have little worth!
O bitter and unfriendly hour!
They've sunk to seventeen and four
From fifty-seven and a quarter!
So poor I am, I'll have to barter
The very garments that I wear...'
He paused, and dropped a salty tear.

Said Mary, 'I should be a freak,
Father, if it didn't break
My heart — or make it fairly ache —
To see you weeping! I've a cache
Of cash conserved indoors! And, sir,
I'm going to marry an Emir!
So dry your eyes at once. Your own
Mary's going to wear a crown!'
The dear girl, much too moved t'await

Her father's answer, rushed to plait
Her horse's tail. He, soon enough,
And after an embarrassed cough,
Pursued her form, so light and lacy,
To the stable's intimacy,
Where, beside the neighing beast,
He unpacked his burdened breast
Of the thanks he owed his daughter.
My story, then, concludes with laughter!

I hope a Mary, reader, thou
Shan't want when down to thy last sou!

William Random
[British]

Homophones

Wood you believe that I didn't no
About homophones until too daze ago?
That day in hour class in groups of for,
We had to come up with won or more.

Mary new six; enough to pass.
But my ate homophones lead the class.
Then a thought ran threw my head.
'Urn a living from homophones,' it said.

I guess I just sat and staired into space.
My hole life seamed to fall into place.
Our school's principle happened to come buy,
And asked about the look in my I.

'Sir,' said I as bowled as could bee,
'My future rode I clearly sea,'
'Sun,' said he, 'move write ahead.
Set sale on your coarse. Don't be misled.'

I herd that gnus with grate delight.
I will study homophones both day and knight.
For weaks and months, through thick oar thin.
I'll pursue my goal. Eye no aisle win.

George E. Coon
[USA]

Typo

"Nitgub," said the typewriter,
And clenched the paper tight.
"Nitgub positively.
It is here in black and white."
"Nonsense," I said.
"I typed N-O-T-H-I-N-G;
The word, of course, was *nothing*,
Simply nothing, don't you see?"
"*Nothing* may be what you meant,
But *nitgub*'s what you wrote.
I like it," said the typewriter.
"It strikes a happy note.
It has more style than *nothing*,
Has a different sort of sound.
The color is superior;
The flavour's nice and round.
Have you plumbed its deepest depths,
Its mystery explained?"
"All right," I said, "I'll take it.
Nitgub ventured, nitgub gained."

Russell Hoban
[USA]

THE ANGUISH OF THE MACHINE

THE HEAT IS ON TOO MUCH PRESSURE PACKING UP
THE HEAT IS ON TOO MUCH PRESSURE PACKING UP
THE HEAT IS ON TOO MUCH PRESSURE PACKING UP
THE HEAT IS ON TOO MUCH PRESSURE PACKING UP
THE HEAT IS ON TOO MUCH PRESSURE PACKING UP
THE HEAT IS ON TOO MUCH PRESSURE PACKING UP
THE HEAT IS ON TOO MUCH PRESSURE PACKING UP

    CAN'T STAND ANY MORE
    CAN'T STAND ANY MORE
    CAN'T STAND ANY MORE   STRAIN TOO GREAT
    CAN'T STAND ANY MORE   STRAIN TOO GREAT
                           STRAIN TOO GREAT

DON'T HAVE A BREAK-   STRAIN TOO GREAT
DOWN DON'T HAVE A   STRAIN TOO GREAT
BREAK-DOWN DON'T H   STRAIN TOO GREAT
AVE A BREAK-
DOWN   DON'T CRACK UP
                       cool down
                       cool down
                       cool down
    don't   cool down
    lose   cool down
    your   cool down
    nerv   cool down
    e   cool down
    don'
    t
    lose
    sto
    pnow

                   don't
                             stop now
       don't

       don't

Peter Murphy
[British]

Orgy

```
cantercantercantercanter
anteateranteateranteater
antencounterantencounter
antennareactantennareact
antantantantantantantant
antantantantantantantant
antantantantantantantant
antantantantantantantant
cantcountantcantcountant
anaccountantanaccountant
anteateranteateranteater
eateateateateateateateat
eateateateateateateateat
anteatenanteatenanteaten
nectarnectarnectarnectar
trancetrancetrancetrance

* * * * * * * * * * * * * * * * * * * * * * * *

canteatanantcanteatanant
anteatercantanteatercant
notanantnotanantnotanant

* * * * * * * * * * * * * * * * * * * * * * * *

trancetrancetrancetrance
ocontentocontentocontent
nocanternocanternocanter
```

Edwin Morgan
[British]

The Hitch-hiker's Curse on Being Passed by

(Excerpts)

The Curse of Your Wheels to you!
May your inlet manifold get choked
While your head gaskets are leaking
And may your camshaft lobes wear out.
Although your cylinders each crack,
A man will be found to replace them,
Wrecking as he does so your valve stem seals
And knocking your tappet clearances awry.
No fruit of your driving: your plugs never dry,
Your tanks never wet — nor those of your daughters.
Trail a long lorry loaded with logs . . .

Speeding to get you nowhere, slowing down
To bring you neither calm nor safety.
Stones to puncture, sheep to stand stubborn
In your path. Dull bulls to dent your doors
As ever forking lanes confound your way.
May your turnings left end all at sea
Unless into quicksand; your rights into mines
Or else onto firing range. May you backfire
And blow the crook from the fist of St Pancras
To bring down all His curses on your neck.
Seven terriers to snarl at your inner tubes.
Rest at last in a black bog, whereupon
A slide of boulders to bury your wheels and you . . .

Crawl, you may as well, up your own silencer,
For be assured: you will come by no agony
But that you will survive to suffer it,
Your fate a mystery to your own people.

John Birtwhistle
[British]

To The Station

'Bye
dear
no, I
won't
drive
fast.
Remember (I keep saying with a
look at the dashboard clock which
is probably a bit slow as usual)
accidents can be
caused by people
like YOU, you dim
blonde crawling Mum
in the middle of the

road with your kinder-
garten-bound load of tod-
dlers. Trouble with (*and* you!)
most motorists they have no
sense of destination, not to say any
feeling for others who are fighting
time
as
they
nip
between wobbly
cyclists and slew-parked
vans, and this sand and gravel
truck suddenly
halting
with
no warning
of any
kind and opens
his
door
and
serve
him
right
if I'd damned-
well killed him. I suppose I can
risk fifty along this bit, no cops

in sight, two minutes to go and I
can make it if I put my foot down
                    and
                    pass
                    this
                    tree-
                    cutting machine
                    on its near
                                side
            a close
        thing, that,

what the hell, I made it. Got
to take a chance now and then
or miss the confounded train, look
out you FOOL in that convertible . . .
                    Hello
                    nurse
                    where am I?

J. R. Boothroyd
[British]

Notes

This section begins with three examples of poets having fun with language. These poems can all be used for some language study without tears: students could find out why, for example, 'wallet' and 'ballet', both borrowings from the French, have different pronunciations. **'Not Enough Dough? Tough!'** must be read aloud.

'The Anguish of the Machine' is an example of concrete poetry. You could try imitating this and the other concrete poems included. In general, poetry uses words arranged into particular patterns to create images, metaphors, rhythm, sound and visual effects. Poets who write concrete poetry have a particular interest in the visual image that the poem creates on the page. Concrete poetry achieves its effects through repetition and word placement which mirrors shape and form.

J. R. Boothroyd's poem is an interesting example of shaped poetry. It could be considered as part of a discussion on 'road rage'. Another readily accessible poem which comments wittily on the road toll is John Betjeman's 'Meditation on the A30'.

Activities

◆ Boothroyd's shaped poem **'To The Station'** invites comparison with **'The Anguish of the Machine'** and **'Orgy'** also included in this section. **'Orgy'** is a clever poem which needs careful line-by-line examination. Photocopy this poem and, with different coloured highlighter pens, mark out the individual words to make them easier to read. Once you marked the poem in this way, prepare an oral presentation of the piece—it could be quite dramatic.

'The Hitch-hiker's Curse on Being Passed by'
◆ Why do people find the need to curse and swear? David Crystal, in *The Cambridge Encyclopedia of the English Language*, suggests a number of reasons: an outlet for frustration, a means of releasing nervous energy after a sudden shock, as a marker of group identity and solidarity, as a way of expressing aggression without resorting to violence. He notes that some people, such as the Polynesians, Amerindians and Japanese, swear very little or not at all; while others, like the Arabs, are famous for the range and imagination of their curses ('You father of sixty dogs' etc.). John Birtwhistle's poem is similarly inventive. Can you write an imaginative curse without resorting to the obscene or the predictable?

Double Exposure

From **The Emigrants**

Columbus from his after-
Deck watched stars, absorbed in water,
Melt in liquid amber drifting

Through my summer air.
Now with morning, shadows lifting,
Beaches stretched before him cold and clear.

Birds circled flapping flag and mizzen
Mast: birds harshly hawking, without fear,
Discovery he sailed for was so near.

Columbus from his after-
Deck watched heights he hoped for,
Rocks he dreamed, rise solid from my simple water.

Parrots screamed. Soon he would touch
Our land, his charted mind's desire.
The blue sky blessed the morning with its fire.

But did his vision
Fashion, as he watched the shore,
The slaughter that his soldiers

Furthered here? Pike
Point and musket butt,
Hot splintered courage, bones

Cracked with bullet shot,
Tipped black boot in my belly, the
Whip's uncurled desire?

Columbus from his after-
Deck saw bearded fig trees, yellow pouis
Blazed like pollen and thin

Waterfalls suspended in the green
As his eyes climbed towards the highest ridges
Where our farms were hidden.

Now he was sure
He heard soft voices mocking in the leaves.
What did this journey mean, this

New world mean: dis-
Covery? Or a return to terrors
He had sailed from, known before?

I watched him pause.

Then he was splashing silence.
Crabs snapped their claws
And scattered as he walked towards our shore.

Edward Brathwaite
[Barbadian]

Catching Crabs

Ruby and me stalking savannah
Crab season with cutlass and sack like big folk.
Hiding behind stones or clumps of bush
Crabs locked knee-deep in mud mating
And Ruby seven years old feeling strange at the sex
And me horrified to pick them up
Plunge them into the darkness of bag,
So all day we scout to catch the lonesome ones
Who don't mind cooking because they got no prospect
Of family, and squelching through the mud,
Cutlass clearing bush at our feet,
We come home tired slow, weighed down with plenty
Which Ma throw live into boiling pot piece-piece.
Tonight we'll have one big happy curry feed,
We'll test out who teeth and jaw strongest
Who will grow up to be the biggest
Or who will make most terrible cannibal.

We leave behind a mess of bones and shell
And come to England and America
Where Ruby hustles in a New York tenement
And me writing poetry at Cambridge,
Death long catch Ma, the house boarded up
Breeding wasps, woodlice in its dark-sack belly:
I am afraid to walk through weed yard,
Reach the door, prise open, look,
In case the pot still bubbles magical
On the fireside, and I see Ma
Working a ladle, slow –
Limbed, crustacean-old, alone,
In case the woodsmoke and curry steam
Burn my child-eye and make it cry.

David Dabydeen
[Guyanan]

They Come for the Islands (1493)

The butchers laid waste the islands.
Guanahani was the first
in that history of torments.
The children of clay saw their
smiles smashed, battered
their stance slight as deers',
all the way to death they did not understand.
They were trussed up and tortured,
they were lit and burned,
they were gnawed and buried.
And when time danced around again
waltzing among the palms
the green hall was empty.

    Nothing was left but bones
    rigidly fastened
    in the form of a cross, to the greater
    glory of God and of men.

    From the chief clay-pits
    and green boughs of Sotavento
    to the coral cays
    the knife of Narváez went carving.
    Here the cross, here the rosary,
    here the Virgin of the Stake.
    Glowing Cuba, Columbus's jewel,
    received the standard and the knees
    in its wet sand.

Pablo Neruda
[Chilean]   *(translated by W. S. Merwin)*

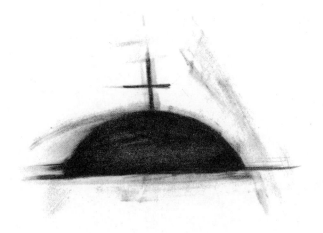

Migrant Woman on a Melbourne Tram

Impossibly black
Amid the impudence of summer thighs
Long arms and painted toenails
And the voices
Impossibly obscure
She hunches sweltering
Twists in sweating hands
A scrap of paper—address, destination,
Clue to the labyrinth
Where voices not understood
Echo
Confusing directions.

    (There was a time
    They sent them out of Greece
    In black-sailed ships
    To feed the minotaur.
    Whose is the blind beast now
    Laired in Collingwood,
    Abbotsford, Richmond,
    Eating up men?)

Street-names in the glare
Leap ungraspably from sight
Formless collisions of letters
Impossibly dark
She is forlorn in foreign words and voices,
Remembering a village
Where poverty was white as bone
And the great silences of sea and sky
Parted at dusk for voices coming home
Calling names
Impossibly departed.

Jennifer Strauss
[Australian]

Immigrants at Central Station, 1951

It was sad to hear
The train's whistle this morning
At the railway station.
All night it had rained.
The air was crowded
With a dampness that slowly
Sank into our thoughts —
But we ate it all:
The silence, the cold, the benevolence
Of empty streets.

Time waited anxiously with us
Behind upturned collars
And space hemmed us
Against each other
Like cattle bought for slaughter.

Families stood
With blankets and packed cases —
Keeping children by their sides,
Watching pigeons
That watched them.

But it was sad to hear
The train's whistle so suddenly —
To the right of our shoulders
Like a word of command.
The signal at the platform's end
Turned red and dropped
Like a guillotine —
Cutting us off from the space of eyesight

While time ran ahead
Along glistening tracks of steel.

Peter Skrzynecki
[Australian]

Notes

E. K. Brathwaite, the Caribbean poet, was born in Bridgetown, Barbados. He is not to be confused with the Guyanan novelist, E. R. Braithwaite, the author of *To Sir with Love*. Chilean poet Pablo Neruda was awarded the Nobel Prize for Literature in 1971. His period of exile in Italy was recently portrayed in the film *Il Postino* (The Postman). Both poems deal with the clash between the 'new' world and the old.

David Dabydeen is a Caribbean poet and academic who was educated in Britain where he now works at the University of Warwick. His poems frequently explore the experience of diaspora, the journey from one culture to another and from the past to the present. The poem **'Catching Crabs'** might prompt you to write about your similar experiences.

Jennifer Strauss lectures in the English Department at Monash University in Melbourne. She has published collections of poems and also edited *The Oxford Book of Australian Love Poetry*.

Peter Skrzynecki, born in Germany in 1945, is of Polish/Ukrainian descent. He came to Australia in 1949 and grew up in Sydney.

Activities

◆ The immigrant experience has been rendered successfully in a number of first-hand accounts contained in *The Immigrants* by Morag Loh and in *Some Came Early, Some Came Late* by Nancy Phelan. One or two such accounts would be excellent starting points for considering the poems by Strauss and Skrzynecki.

◆ In your group, collect some stories of migrant experiences, either from friends and relatives or from books like *The Immigrants*. Then plan, record on cassette and present a program on such experiences, incorporating a reading of one of the poems in your presentation.

◆ Write a description of an unusual person you have observed when travelling on public transport.

◆ Improvise and then write a script of a conversation between two or more people you have overheard while travelling on public transport.

◆ **'Migrant Woman on a Melbourne Tram'** might also be read in conjunction with Katherine Gallagher's poem **'Passengers to the City'** (page 57) and included in the activity in which you try to capture in writing a stranger you have observed while travelling.

Indigenous Images

Bran Nue Day

This fella song
All about the Aboriginal people
Coloured people, black people along Australia.
Us people want our land back,
We want'em rights
We want'em fair deal
All same longa white man.

Now this fella longa Canberra
He bin talkin' about a Bran Nue Day
Us people bin waiting for dijwun*
for two hundred years now.

Don' know how much more we gotta wait
and boy it's making me slack.

Here I live in this tin shack
Nothing here worth coming back
To drunken fights and awful sights
People drunk most every night.

On the way to a Bran Nue Day
Everybody everybody say.
On the way to a Bran Nue Day
Everybody everybody say.

Other day I bin longa to social security,
I bin ask longa job—
They bin say, "Hey what's your work experience?"
I bin tell'em, "I got nothing."
They say, "How come?"
I say, "'Cause I can't find a job."

*This one

We've nothing old, and nothing new
Want us all to be like you.
We've no future we have no past
Hope the sun will shine at last.

On the way to a Bran Nue Day
Everybody everybody say.
On the way to Bran Nue Day
Everybody everybody say.

On the way to a Bran Nue Day
Everybody everybody say.
On the way to a Bran Nue Day
Everybody everybody say.

Jimmy Chi & Mick Manolis
[Australian]

We Are Going

For Grannie Coolwell

They came in to the little town
A semi-naked band subdued and silent,
All that remained of their tribe.
They came here to the place of their old bora ground
Where now the many white men hurry about
     like ants.
Notice of estate agent reads: "Rubbish May Be
Tipped Here."
Now it half covers the traces of the old bora ring.
They sit and are confused, they cannot say their
     thoughts:
"We are as strangers here now, but the white tribe
     are the strangers.
We belong here, we are of the old ways.
We are the corroboree and the bora ground.
We are the old sacred ceremonies, the laws of
     the elders.
We are the wonder tales of Dreamtime, the tribal
     legends told.
We are the past, the hunts and the laughing games,
     the wandering camp fires.
We are the lightning-bolt over Gaphembah Hill
Quick and terrible.
And the Thunderer after him, that loud fellow.
We are the quiet daybreak paling the dark lagoon.

We are the shadow-ghosts creeping back as the
    camp fires burn low.
We are nature and the past, all the old ways
Gone now and scattered."

Oodgeroo Noonuccal
[Australian]

Whitefellas

Whitefellas are rich
Whitefellas have new cars
Whitefellas wear clean clothes
Tourists come out, look round my country,
find gold or something,
go back, spread 'em word
Whitefellas run settlement,
properly, do it proper way
Whitefellas say:
"we're going to Alice Springs" but
talk talk talk talk
waste time, maybe one hour
Whitefellas talk too much
sometime lie,
sometime true
Whitefellas talk mean
Whitefellas cheat, say:
"this *good* car!"
Whitefellas got strange eyes
Tourists don't care
they look funny
women wear shorts too tight
Whitefellas got no shame
Whitefellas don't turn back
because they're millionaires
Whitefellas complain too much
about everything—even other Whitefellas
Whitefellas don't help each other
Whitefellas take photo without asking
Whitefellas stare
Whitefellas don't feel
anything.

The Post-Primary Boys' Class
Papunya School,
Papunya Settlement,
Northern Territory
[Australian]

Mimi Dancers

From out of the spirit world
they all came dancing,
the seven spirit brothers
and the seven sisters,
the mimi spirits from space.
Down through the Milky Way they danced
to the earth far below.
They came to dance among the mountains,
in the rivers as they wound
    their way to the sea.
They danced across the cliff face,
    the mimi spirits from space.
They danced of life for the plans to unfold,
    the mimi spirits from space.
They danced upon the earth,
they danced upon the rocks,
they danced upon the bark
and they danced upon the canvas,
    the mimi spirits from space.
They danced on the limbs of the trees,
    in the rustling of the leaves.
They danced in the wind for everlasting life.
They danced the dreaming alive,
    the mimi spirits from space.

Lorraine Mafi-Williams
[Australian]

The Curlew Cried

Three nights they heard the curlew cry.
It is the warning known of old
That tells them one tonight shall die.

Brother and friend, he comes and goes
Out of the Shadow Land to them,
The loneliest voice that earth knows.

He guards the welfare of his own,
He comes to lead each soul away —
To what dim world, what strange unknown?

Who is it that tonight must go:
The old blind one? The cripple child?
Tomorrow all the camp will know.

The poor dead will be less afraid,
Their tribe brother will be with him
When the dread journey must be made.

'Have courage, death is not an end,'
He seems to say. 'Though you must weep,
Death is kindly and is your friend.'

Three nights the curlew cried. Once more
He comes to take the timorous dead —
To what grim change, what ghostly shore?

Oodgeroo Noonuccal
[Australian]

Notes

This group of poems captures the voices, images and traditions of indigenous Australians. In several of the poems the poets regret the loss or dispossession of their land and of the traditions and stories that were connected to the land. The first three poems in this section provide an Aboriginal perspective on the promises and behaviours of White people. The clash of values and the consequences for the Aboriginal people are central concerns. But not all these poems are sad: **'Mimi Dancers'** is about the lively spirit people who created the Dreaming; **'Whitefellas'** gives White Australians a humorous chance to look at themselves from a different point of view.

'Bran Nue Day'

dijwun—this one

The poem/song lyrics rely on the irony of the kind of **'Bran Nue Day'** that is dawning for the Aboriginal people. Jimmy Chi (a self-taught musician) and the Kuckles band devised the first major Aboriginal musical, *Bran Nue Day*, from which this poem is taken. The musical is set in Broome in northern Western Australia and is a celebration of the place of music in the life of the city. The music in the performance draws on many musical styles: an amalgam of reggae, gospel, country, rock, which has tremendous vitality. The performance and the songs compel the audience to identify with the plight of the characters and to celebrate their capacity to survive. In the musical performance the audience sings the chorus of the lyrics and in doing so succumbs to its uncompromising message. The musical is available on video and compact disc. The script has also been published by Currency Press, 1991.

'We Are Going'

bora ground—a circular ring of stones on a tribal ceremonial ground where important initiation rituals were celebrated through traditional dance and song

The Thunderer—The Thunder man, Jambuwal, is an important ancestral being of some of the people in north-eastern Arnhem Land. Like the Lightning man, Namarrkon, he is often represented in rock and bark paintings. Dreaming stories provide accounts of his anger which he expresses in storm clouds and rough seas.

Oodgeroo Noonuccal is an Australian poet. Noonuccal is the name of the Aboriginal people of Minjerribah (Stradbroke Island). Oodgeroo is her first, or totemic, name. It means paperbark tree. As the custodian of Minjerribah, for years she has written poetry about her people. Her early poems were published under the name 'Kath Walker'. Her poems and writings often record the legends of her people. She explains:

> Our legends are our bond between our Earth Mother, the sea, and the sky. Between ourselves and our tribespeople, between the living and the dead,

between all living things. We are rich in spite of the stolen lands, in spite of the racists, in spite of being dispossessed, for our legends keep us alive, warm and happy.

(*Legends and Landscapes*, Random House, 1990).

'Whitefellas'

Papunya—Papunya is in Central Australia and is the home of the now familiar dot paintings that were originally painted in the desert sand.

'Mimi Dancers'

mimi—The mimis were believed to be creation spirits who were also exceptionally skilled spirit hunters. They first taught Aboriginals how to use spears. Their images are widespread in Aboriginal rock art in Arnhem Land. They often appear as slim, athletic, moving figures, hunting, spearing, running or dancing. According to Ronald and Catherine Berndt, who have collected Aboriginal myths and stories in the Western Desert, Arnhem Land, west-central Northern Territory and the Kimberleys, they are 'non-human, stick-like creatures who are said to live among the rocks of the escarpment country'. You may have seen photographs of rock paintings in books in which the mimi are depicted as 'all skin and bones, naked stick-like creatures with big heads and hair'. (See Ronald M. Berndt & Catherine H. Berndt 1989, *The Speaking Land*, Penguin, Ringwood.)

Lorraine Mafi-Williams describes herself as a film-maker, writer, social activist, teacher and cultural ambassador. She is a descendent of the Thungatti tribe and Bandjalang tribes and was instructed in the teachings of the Githraubaul tribe by her grandmother and her aunt.

'The Curlew Cried'

The curlew (a bird) is a 'taciturn and gloomy fellow' whose cries 'echo mournfully'. Although seen by some Aboriginal tribes as a brother, the curlew's cry near a camp three nights in succession was taken as providing a sign of an impending death. It was believed that the curlew came to lead the shadow of the dead one away to the unknown world.

Activities

◆ A good way to explore the poems is to study them in a small group and prepare a performance or oral reading of them. Experiment with different readings and different groupings of the poems to capture their contrasting moods. **'Bran Nue Day'** is a song from the musical of the same name.

◆ Try to locate the CD (or video) and present the sung version. You could pair it with **'Whitefellas'** to emphasise its upbeat quality, or with **'We Are Going'** to highlight the theme of loss.

◆ Can you work out a way to link **'The Curlew Cried'** and **'Mimi Dancers'**?

The Oral Tradition

The 'word' of an antelope caught in a trap

I dwell on the misty steppe.
I belong to Manakhan, the Lord of the Beasts.
In the deep cold of winter,
In the blinding snow-storms,
I went of my own accord
To gentler, warmer pastures.
With the changing season
I went frolicking along
With my myriad companions,
To return to our old pastures.
Through the power of former deeds
I was caught in a snare.
My twenty myriad companions,
Forming a wedge, vanished from sight,
And I, bereft of my heel-tendons,
Fell behind, gazing after them.
My hundred myriad companions,
Neck and neck, vanished from sight,
And I, caught in the middle of my way,
Fell behind, to endure my pain.
My many myriad companions
Went off, straight in line,
And I, caught in the toils,
Fell behind, to await death.
To be hunted
Is the way of the world
May I find a peaceful new birth,
Transcending the state of the wild beast.

Sandag
[Mongolian]

Leopard

Gentle hunter
His tail plays on the ground
While he crushes the skull.

Beautiful death
Who puts on a spotted robe
When he goes to his victim.

Playful killer
Whose loving embrace
Splits the antelope's heart.

Yoriba poetry
[Nigerian]

Three songs from the Moon-Bone cycle

In the *jiridja* cycle of the Moon-Bone the Moon lived with his sister Dugong in the ancient Dream time. They collected Lily and Lotus Roots, symbolically associated with the Evening Star. The Moon eventually travelled out to sea, cast his bone into the water, and after three days climbed up into the sky. Now every month he repeats this: he throws his bone into the ssea, where it becomes the nautilus shell, and is born again. In the last song the Evening Star is revealed as a Lotus Bloom and a Lily Root, and the string attached to it is the stalk of these plants.

The birds

The birds saw the people walking along.
Crying, the white cockatoos flew over the clay pan of the Moonlight;

From the place of the Dugong they flew, looking for lily-root
    food; pushing the foliage down and eating the soft roots.
Crying, the birds flew down and along the clay pan, at that
    place of the Dugong ...
Crying, flying down there along the clay pan ...
At the place of the Dugong, of the Tree-Limbs-Rubbing-
    Together, and of the Evening Star.
Where the lily-root clay pan is ...
Where the cockatoos play, at that pace of the Dugong ...
Flapping their wings they flew down, crying, 'We saw the
    people!'
There they are always living, those clans of the white cockatoo ...
And there is the Shag woman, and there her clan:
Birds, trampling the lily foliage, eating the soft round roots!

New Moon

Now the New Moon is hanging, having cast away his bone:
Gradually he grows larger, taking on new bone and flesh.
Over there, far away, he has shed his bone: he shines on the
        place of the Lotus Root, and the place of the Dugong,
On the place of the Evening Star, of the Dugong's Tail, of the
        Moonlight clay pan . . .
His old bone gone, now the New Moon grows larger;
Gradually growing, his new bone growing as well.
Over there, the horns of the old receding Moon bent down,
        sank into the place of the Dugong:
His horns were pointing towards the place of the Dugong.
Now the New Moon swells to fullness, his bone grown larger,
He looks on the water, hanging above it, at the place of the
        Lotus.
There he comes into sight, hanging above the sea, growing
        larger and older . . .
There far away he has come back, hanging over the clans near
        Milingimbi . . .
Hanging there in the sky, above those clans . . .
'Now I'm becoming a big moon, slowly regaining my roundness . . .'
In the far distance the horns of the Moon bend down, above
        Milingimbi,
Hanging a long way off, above Milingimbi Creek . . .
Slowly the Moon-Bone is growing, hanging there far away.
The bone is shining, the horns of the Moon bend down.
First the sickle Moon on the old Moon's shadow; slowly he
        grows,
And shining he hangs there at the place of the Evening Star . . .
Then far away he goes sinking down, to lose his bone in the sea;
Diving towards the water, he sinks down out of sight.
The old Moon dies to grow new again, to rise up out of the sea.

The Evening Star

Up and up soars the Evening Star, hanging there in the sky.
Men watch it, at the place of the Dugong and of the Clouds, and
        of the Evening Star,
A long way off, at the place of Mist, of Lilies and of the Du-
        gong.
The Lotus, the Evening Star, hangs there on its long stalk, held
        by the Spirits.
It shines on that place of the Shade, on the Dugong place, and
        on to the Moonlight clay pan . . .
The Evening Star is shining, back towards Milingimbe, and over
        the 'Wulamba people . . .

Hanging there in the distance, towards the place of the Dugong,
The place of the Eggs, of the Tree-Limbs-Rubbing-Together,
        and of the Moonlight clay pan . . .
Shining on its short stalk, the Evening Star, always there at the
      clay pan, at the place of the Dugong . . .
There, far away, the long string hangs at the place of the
      Evening Star, the place of Lilies.

Away there at Milingimbi . . . at the place of the Full Moon,
Hanging above the head of that *'Wonguri* tribesman:
The Evening Star goes down across the camp, among the white
      gum trees . . .
Far away, in those places near Milingimbi . . .
Goes down among the *'Nurulwulu* people, towards the camp and
      the gum trees,
At the place of the Crocodiles, and of the Evening Star, away
      towards Milingimbi . . .
The Evening Star is going down, the Lotus Flower on its
      stalk . . .
Going down among all those western clans . . .
It brushes the heads of the uncircumcised people . . .
Sinking down in the sky, that Evening Star, the Lotus . . .
Shining on to the foreheads of all those headmen . . .
On to the heads of all those Sandfly people . . .
It sinks there into the place of the white gum trees, at Milin-
      gimbi.

[Australian]

Notes

This section is designed to illustrate the rich heritage of oral poetry character-istic of many, if not most cultures. While we associate oral or unwritten poetry chiefly with pre-literate or semi-literate societies, one thinks of Aboriginal tribes or the Celtic bards or the medieval wandering minstrels—it is worth remem-bering that minority groups in modern European cultures have produced their own oral poetry. For example, the protest songs of British and US coal miners, and the songs of the Irish protesting against British rule.

'The 'word' of an antelope caught in a trap'
This poem is attributed to a minstrel called Sandag who lived in Mongolia in the nineteenth century. He and other members of his tribe produced a number of 'word' poems which you could try imitating. These are essentially improvisa-tions upon a theme, in which the subject, usually an animal, comments on the fate that has overtaken it. (See also *The Penguin Book of Oral Poetry*, ed. Ruth Finnegan.)

'Leopard'
This is a poem from the Yoruba tribe of Nigeria.

'The Moon-Bone cycle'
This is one of the many song cycles from the indigenous people from Arnhem Land. Each part is a complete song rather than a verse of a longer poem; some of the song cycles have as many as two or three hundred parts.

Activities

◆ See if you can locate examples of the protest songs made up by the British and US coal miners during the period when they were faced with the loss of their jobs resulting from mine closures.

◆ In the late 1960s and early 1970s, US song writers and protest singers were influential in drawing attention to major social issues and problems. Can you compile a list of singer/songwriters who are fulfilling that role now? What are the 'hot' issues they are writing songs about?

◆ Use **'Leopard'** and/or **'The 'word' of an antelope caught in a trap'** as a model to write your own poem about a domestic or wild animal whose habits you know well.

$\mathcal{P}$oems and Pictures

The Cricketers

(after the painting by Russell Drysdale, 1948)

A boy bowls up on the edge of the red sand.
Beyond that — desert with no boundary
for a six. A full toss into the swung
shadow on a wall of sun. Patiently

a boy at point leans on the hot iron
verandah post that throws no shade. Either
way has little to catch. Will take his turn
with bat and ball in the cycle of their

game: not played for runs but hours. There
is only one crease: a few piles of stone
built places that stand on fringes where
drought years are a long slow drive beyond.

Spectators in an empty land pitching
hopelessly into the heart of nothing.

Jeff Guess
[Australian]

How to Paint the Portrait of a Bird

First paint a cage
with an open door
then paint
something pretty
something simple
something fine
something useful
for the bird
next place the canvas against a tree
in a garden
in a wood
or in a forest
hide behind the tree
without speaking
without moving . . .
Sometimes the bird comes quickly
but it can take many years
before making up its mind
Don't be discouraged
wait
wait if necessary for years
the quickness or the slowness of the coming
of the bird having no relation
to the success of the picture
When the bird comes
if it comes
observe the deepest silence
wait for the bird to enter the cage
and when if has entered
gently close the door with the paint-brush
then
one by one paint-out all the bars
taking care not to touch one feather of the bird
Next make a portrait of the tree
choosing the finest of its branches
for the bird
paint also the green leaves and the freshness of the wind
dust in the sun
and the sound of the grazing cattle in the heat of summer
and wait for the bird to decide to sing
If the bird does not sing
it is a bad sign
a sign that the picture is bad
but if it sings it is a good sign
a sign that you are ready to sign

so then you pluck very gently
one of the quills of the bird
and you write your name in a corner of the picture.

Jacques Prévert
[French]   *(translated by Paul Dehn)*

Giorgio de Chirico

It is always late afternoon
in the abandoned square.

The pennants are streaming out
though there is no wind,

the sky has darkened early
to a murky electric indigo

and the proud equestrian statue,
lit from a strange angle,

is struck with a shadow
as shapeless as a corpse.

Beyond the uniform white arcades,
beyond the distant red tower

there is an approaching rhythm:
the crunching sound of jackboots.

Philip Hodgins
[Australian]

Man Lying on a Wall

Homage to L. S. Lowry

You could draw a straight line from the heels,
Through calves, buttocks and shoulderblades
To the back of the head: pressure points
That bear the enormous weight of the sky.
Should you take away the supporting structure
The result would be a miracle or
An extremely clever conjuring trick.
As it is, the man lying on the wall
Is wearing the serious expression
Of popes and kings in their final slumber,
His deportment not dissimilar to
Their stiff, reluctant exits from this world
Above the shoulders of the multitude.

It is difficult to judge whether or not
He is sleeping or merely disinclined
To arrive punctually at the office
Or to return home in time for his tea.
He is wearing a pinstripe suit, black shoes
And a bowler hat: on the pavement
Below him, like a relic or something
He is trying to forget, his briefcase
With everybody's initials on it.

Michael Longley
[British]

Paring the Apple

There are portraits and still-lifes.

And there is paring the apple.

And then? Paring it slowly,
From under cool-yellow
Cold-white emerging. And . . .?

The spring of concentric peel
Unwinding off white,
The blade hidden, dividing.

There are portraits and still-lifes
And the first, because 'human'
Does not excel the second, and
Neither is less weighted
With a human gesture, than paring the apple
With a human stillness.

The cool blade
Severs between coolness, apple-rind
Compelling a recognition.

Charles Tomlinson
[British]

Notes

The poems and pictures in this section are connected in an obvious way, in that the poems have been written in response to each of the paintings. While there is a direct relationship between each poem and the accompanying picture, each poem and artwork should be able to stand alone. Do the pictures make the poems richer and more meaningful? Do the poems add anything to the pictures? Can the poems stand alone, or do they need the paintings to be fully understood? How do the poems interpret what we see in the pictures?

Artists and writers are often asked how they get their ideas, how they choose their subjects, and how they go about writing, creating a picture or musical composition, etc. The notion that artists are inspired and that their ideas seem to come to them fully formed from out of nowhere, not only is inaccurate, but also does not helpfully inform those wishing to learn about making art.

Artists, writers, musicians and performers carefully study and creatively draw upon the work of other artists, across a range of disciplines and media. Visual artists, writers, dancers and musicians all produce their 'original' works from a range of influences from other artists. They use the work of others as models for solving technical problems, and as springboards from which to make something new.

While the poets in this section have written in response to a picture, the painters of those pictures have themselves drawn on the work of other artists for their themes, images and ideas. For instance, in painting *The Cricketers*, Russell Drysdale was deeply influenced by Giorgio de Chirico's paintings. A postcard-size reproduction of the picture *Piazza d'Italia* (1913) was for many years pinned to the wall of Drysdale's studio. He had previously seen and studied many of de Chirico's paintings, and was particularly interested in de Chirico's management of shadow and the balance of light and dark in his pictures.

Similarly, the lonely odd little figure lying on a wall in L. S. Lowry's painting owes much to the artist's interest in the lonely, odd little figures created by the legendary comedian Charles Chaplin in his silent films. Chaplin's comic figures were recognisable by their big boots, bowler hats and umbrellas. Lowry identified with these hapless figures; the briefcase in the picture even has Lowry's initials, 'L. S. L.', written on the side.

'The Cricketers'

Jeff Guess (b. 1948) is an Australian poet who was born and educated in South Australia. He is a secondary school teacher with a deep interest in the history of his state, and the place where he lives. He has written a number of volumes of poetry.

The process by which the painter Russell Drysdale (1912–81) made *The Cricketers* is revealing of the work, thought, influences, and energy that go into creating a picture of this quality. In 1948 Drysdale began painting a series of pictures incorporating aspects of the scenes around the New South Wales country town of Hill End. The building against which the boys are playing cricket is the old hotel in the town. Drysdale did many realistic pencil sketches as he collected images for the painting—drawings of the boys batting and bowling, others of an elongated youth in a desolate landscape with the hotel in the background, studies of the buildings, and so on. That the boys in the picture are playing cricket is no accident. Drysdale was a cricket fanatic. As a boy in Geelong he was known by the nickname, 'Blocky', and was renowned for carrying a cricket bat wherever he went. By focusing on the boys playing a 'backyard' cricket match into the last few minutes of daylight, the picture is celebrating cricket, as much as it is rendering Drysdale's vision of the foreboding Australian landscape. The emptiness of Drysdale's landscapes was also deliberate. He was reacting against the sense of security that earlier Australian painters had created in their paintings. The paintings of Tom Roberts are a good example. Drysdale was not interested in rendering the bright freshness of light in the Australian landscape, nor in making the figures in the landscape seem as if they belonged there. He changed the nature of the way Australians saw the landscape by making it more gloomy, pessimistic and alien. The figures in his paintings are not at home in the landscape, they are alien to it.

We can see the influence of Giorgio de Chirico in the way Drysale elongates the shadows and uses the space between the buildings to emphasise the figures. The picture owes more to de Chirico than it does to the earlier tradition of Australian landscape painting.

'How to Paint the Portrait of a Bird'
Jacques Prévert (1900–77) was a French writer of prose and poetry. Much of his work is humorous and satirical. It was written in response to Braque's picture *The Bird*.

Georges Braque (1882–1963) and Pablo Picasso (1881–1973) are credited with creating the art movement known as Cubism. Cubism was a radical departure from established art practices in the early twentieth century. It employed angular shapes, a flattening of space, and blocks of colour. The technique then used to represent things as they appear in perspective gave way in Cubism to a flattened representation of objects from various perspectives at the same time in the one compositional space. These artists attempted to express the *idea* of an object rather than to simply present a view of it. Cubism was heavily influenced by Negro and North African art practices, particularly sculpture.

'Man Lying on a Wall'
Michael Longley (b. 1939) was born and lives in Northern Ireland. He was a secondary school teacher until he was made Director of Literature and the

The Cricketers by Russell Drysdale

Man Lying on a wall by L. S. Lowry

The Bird by Georges Braque

Woman Peeling Apples by Peter de Hoogh

The Great Game (Italian Square) by Giorgio de Chirico

Traditional Arts at the Arts Council of Northern Ireland. He has a deep sympathy with the animal world and his poems contain a great variety of creatures.

Laurence Stephen Lowry (1887–1976) was born in Manchester, England, and lived there all his life. He painted industrial and slum landscapes inhabited by diminutive stick figures and eccentric characters. Of himself and his work Lowry once said in an interview: 'I am a simple man, and I use simple materials; ivory black, vermillion, prussian blue, yellow ochre, flake white—and no medium. That's all I've ever used for my painting. I like oils . . . I like a media you can work *into*, over a period of time'.

'Paring the Apple'

Charles Tomlinson (b. 1927) is a British poet and academic whose writing has been heavily influenced by contemporary US writers. He is widely published. He is also a visual artist. An ability to observe minute details and to render these in exactly the right words gives his poetry a unique quality. In commenting on his own writing he once observed: 'My theme is relationship. The hardness of crystals, the facets of cut glass; but also the shifting of light, the energising weather which is the result of the combination of sun and frost—these are the images for a certain mental climate, components for the moral landscape of my poetry in general.'

Pieter de Hooch (1629–84) was a Dutch painter of considerable skill and influence. His paintings are recognised for their elaborate space construction, use of light, and warm colours (deep reds, blacks, blues, greys, and yellows). He masterfully captures the tender feelings which radiate from the homely, domestic figures of his art.

'Giorgio de Chirico'

Philip Hodgins (1959–95) was an Australian poet. Other poems by him are to be found in the sections Action Shots, Landscapes and Still Life and Reptilian Adventures of this volume. Although one picture by de Chirico, *The Great Game (Italian Square)*, 1971, is included in this section, it would appear that Hodgins did not have a particular painting in mind when he wrote his poem.

Giorgio de Chirico (1888–1978) was an Italian painter, born in Greece of Italian parents. He was trained as a painter in Athens (Greece), Munich (Germany), Paris (France), and Italy. His paintings are immediately recognisable— strangely distorted views of uninhabited cityscapes: statues in deserted squares; darkened, gloomy skies; angular shapes and buildings; and extended, elongated shadows.

Activities

◆ From Philip Hodgins' poem see if you can make some sketches representing the images he describes. Do not be concerned about the size of the picture—a page from a normal exercise book is enough.

◆ Once you have done some sketches, see if you can locate one of the many books that have been written about Giorgio de Chirico, in which you will find reproductions of his work.

◆ Having looked at a range of pictures, you can see that the elements identified by Philip Hodgins are repeated over and over again in de Chirico's paintings from a certain period. You can probably also see why Russell Drysdale was so interested in his use of shadow to create a sense of foreboding.

Variations and Special Effects

Summary of a Western

We see a dusty desert scene and that's
The way the film begins. Some men in hats
Deliver gritty lines. They all wear braces.
They're cool and tough. They hate the darker races
Who paint peculiar stripes across their faces.

Goodies meet baddies, mostly in corrals.
Cowboys ignore or patronise their gals.
We see a gun twirl in a macho hand.
Who's killing whom we don't quite understand —
There's always some vague reference to the land.

Women in aprons have to be protected.
Stagecoaches fall. New sheriffs are elected.
The cast consists primarily of horses —
They gallop to the ending, which of course is
A happy one, where nobody divorces.

Sophie Hannah
[British]

The Horse That Had a Flat Tire

Once upon a valley
there came down
from some goldenblue mountains
a handsome young prince
who was riding
a dawncolored horse
named Lordsburg.

> I love you
> You're my breathing castle
> Gentle so gentle
> We'll live forever

In the valley
there was a beautiful maiden
whom the prince
drifted into love with
like a New Mexico made from
apple thunder and long
glass beds.

> I love you
> You're my breathing castle
> Gentle so gentle
> We'll live forever

The prince enchanted
the maiden
and they rode off
on the dawncolored horse
named Lordsburg
toward the goldenblue mountains.

> I love you
> You're my breathing castle
> Gentle so gentle
> We'll live forever

They would have lived
happily ever after
if the horse hadn't had
a flat tire
in front of a dragon's house.

Richard Brautigan
[USA]

You'd Better Believe Him—A Fable

Discovered an old rocking-horse in Woolworth's,
He tried to feed it but without much luck
So he stroked it, had a long conversation about
The trees it came from, the attics it had visited.
Tried to take it out then
But the store detective he
Called the store manager who
Called the police who in the court next morning said
'He acted strangely when arrested,
His statement read simply "I believe in rocking-horses."
We have reason to believe him mad.'
'Quite so,' said the prosecution,
'Bring in the rocking horse as evidence.'
'I'm afraid it's escaped sir,' said the store manager,
'Left a hoof-print as evidence
On the skull of the store detective.'
'Quite so,' said the prosecution, fearful
Of the neighing
Out in the corridor.

Brian Patten
[British]

The Waiting Wolf

First, I saw her feet
beneath a red pointed cloak
head bent forward
parting the woods,
one foot placed straight
in front of the other.

Then, came her scent.
I was meant to stalk her
smooth, not a twig snaps.
It is the only way I know.
I showed her flowers—
white dead-nettle, nightshade.
devil's bit, wood anemone.

I might not have gone further,
but then nothing ever remains
innocent in the woods.

When she told me about Grandmother,
I sickened. She placed herself on my path,
practically spilling her basket of breads and jams.

Waiting in this old lady's ruffled bed.
I am all calculation. I have gone this far —
dressed in Grandmother's lace panties,
flannel nightgown and cap,
puffs of breath beneath the sheet
lift and fall. I can see my heart tick.
Slightly. Slightly.

These are small lies for a wolf,
but strangely heavy in my belly like stones.
I will forget them as soon as I have her,
still, at this moment I do not like myself.

When she crawls into Grandma's bed,
will she pull me close, thinking:
This is my grandmother whom I love?

She will have the youngest skin
I have ever touched, her fingers unfurling
My matted fur will smell to her of forest
moss at night. She'll wonder about my ears,
large, pointed, soft as felt,
my eyes red as her cloak,
my leather nose on her belly.

But perhaps she has known who I am since the first,
since we took the other path
through the woods.

Gwen Strauss
[USA]

Sleeping Snow-White

There must have been a girl once
who lay in a coma for many days,
her eyelids locked, her imperceptible
heartbeat holding off corruption.

A princess, or at any rate highborn,
for the misfortunes of peasants weren't remarkable
(they lived and suffered unseen in their hovels) —
while everybody knew about this girl

and looked for ways to wake her.
Perhaps the story's true end
is that she died, stopped breathing
in her sleep without a struggle.

A conclusion to be rebelled against —
rather the fiction and the prince,
an awakening for all of us who're good
and beautiful enough.

Pamela Gillilan
[British]

The Other Version (1)

Our Freda had a nasty experience the other night.
Down there by the river, where it's lonely.
You know the place. I always say they ought to put
Some lights there. Well, up loomed one of those
Horrid princes. We all know what they're like,
Oh yes we do. Great big uglies, nothing's safe
When they're around. Clumsy brutes, and cheeky
With it. I can't abide them. The very thought
Brings on my asthma.

Well, this prince comes out with a tale about how
He was really a frog. One of us if he had his rights.
A likely story, I don't think! And if only Freda
Would be kind enough to — you know what he was after,
Only one thought in their heads — then he would turn
      back
Into a frog. Something to do with an old witch.
He must have thought young Freda was dopier than she
      is.
"Witches!" she hoots. "Don't give me none of that
Stuff and nonsense. Everybody knows they don't exist."
Then she said she'd screech her head off if he didn't
Beat it pronto. Which he did.

Freda said after, if he hadn't tried to get round her
With that soppy story — if he'd been straight with her —
Then maybe she'd have seen her way. Some of them
Aren't so bad, she said, you got to take them as you
Find them, they can't help being princes . . . Speechless
I was. But you know what young frogs are like these days.

D. J. Enright
[British]

The Other Version (2)

You want the true story? Very well.
As a young man, I couldn't find work here —
My size didn't help, as you can imagine.
So I went abroad.

The natives of the country I went to
Were an idle lot, no initiative at all,
Except for getting themselves into silly
Unprofitable scrapes.

Like this girl I bumped into one day.
She was in trouble. If she hadn't been,
I don't suppose she would have noticed me.
The people there eyed me askance,
Because of my foreign accent, as well as my —
Well, my handicap.

The girl was certainly in a mess.
Some country squire, a layabout like the rest,
Had promised to do the right thing by her
As long as she could spin straw into gold.

I'd always thought there was money in straw,
Plenty of it lying around, going for a song.
So I lent her a hand, and before very long
We were showing a handsome profit. Then
This fellow was only too glad to marry her,
You can bet!

She wanted to pay me back for my help,
She wasn't a bad sort really. And this gave rise
To malicious gossip, all of it untrue.
So I said jokingly, "Let's see if you can
Get my name right. Then we'll call it quits."

D. J. Enright
[British]

Nursery Rhyme of Innocence and Experience

I had a silver penny
    And an apricot tree
And I said to the sailor
    On the white quay

'Sailor O sailor
    Will you bring me
If I give you my penny
    And my apricot tree

'A fez from Algeria
    An Arab drum to beat
A little gilt sword
    And a parakeet?'

And he smiled and he kissed me
    As strong as death
And I saw his red tongue
    And I felt his sweet breath

'You may keep your penny
    And your apricot tree
And I'll bring your presents
    Back from sea.'

O the ship dipped down
    On the rim of the sky
And I waited while three
    Long summers went by

Then one steel morning
    On the white quay
I saw a grey ship
    Come in from sea

Slowly she came
    Across the bay
For her flashing rigging
    Was shot away

All round her wake
    The seabirds cried
And flew in and out
    Of the hole in her side

Slowly she came
    In the path of the sun
And I heard the sound
    Of a distant gun

And a stranger came running
    Up to me
From the deck of the ship
    And he said, said he

'O *are you the boy*
    Who would wait on the quay
With the silver penny
    And the apricot tree?

'*I've a plum-coloured fez*
    And a drum for thee
And a sword and a parakeet
    From over the sea.'

'O where is the sailor
    With bold red hair?
And what is that volley
    On the bright air?

'O where are the other
    Girls and boys?
And why have you brought me
    Children's toys?'

Charles Causley
[British]

Notes

'The Horse That Had a Flat Tire' and 'You'd Better Believe Him—A Fable' complement each other well. Their unusual vision of events manages to illuminate briefly the question of sanity and reality. Brautigan's retelling of a familiar story is all the more attractive with its bizarre ending. A horse with a flat tyre, indeed!

Gwen Strauss's poem is taken from a collection of hers entitled *Trail of Stones* (Julia MacRae Books). Each of the poems in the collection explores traditional fairy tales from unusual perspectives.

In *Postcards from Planet Earth*, the companion volume to *Snapshots of Planet Earth*, you will find Liz Lochhead's *Rapunzstiltskin*, a reworking of the Rapunzel story.

The section ends with a Charles Causley ballad with echoes of both nursery rhymes and folk tales. It might be paired with Ted Hughes's **'Leaves'** (page 130), which is based quite directly on *Who Killed Cock Robin?*

Activities

◆ Discuss **'The Horse that Had a Flat Tire'** and **'You'd Better Believe Him'** and decide what the moral behind the two poems is.

◆ After reading **'The Waiting Wolf'** try retelling a well-known fairy story from the point of view of a different character.

◆ Put the wolf from Gwen Strauss's **'The Waiting Wolf'** on trial. What justifications does he offer for attacking Little Red Riding Hood?

◆ After reading D. J. Enright's two poems, try to write a humorous 'other version'.

◆ Many poets and novelists have reworked the themes and plots of fairy stories and folk tales, perhaps because such tales deal with universal concerns. (Think how many novels and films are basically reworkings of *Cinderella*.) This section contains four such reworkings.

◆ Read the following passage, from the beginning of a short story by Clodagh Corcoran and try some of the follow-up activities. The story is based on the fairy tale of *Snow White and the Seven Dwarfs* and is written as if it is a newspaper report of a court case involving the various participants in the fairy tale.

Ms Snow White Wins Case in High Court

In a landmark decision handed down in Court yesterday by Ms Justice Goodbye, Snow White was granted an injunction against seven men. Mark Miword reports on the case.

> Snow White was yesterday granted an injunction in the High Court in Dublin, restraining a total of seven men from entering on or interfering with the premises in the heart of the woods, which had been shared between them for ten years. The Court heard how Ms White had been abused for a total of ten years by the defendants, since she was seven years old. In an extempore judgement, Ms Justice Goodbye said that it was the worst case she had ever been forced to hear . . .

(from Susan Adler (ed.) 1990, *Mightier Than the Lipstick, Stories by Women*, Viking.)

◆ Collect some examples of court reports from major capital city newspapers. Read them carefully to ensure that you have a grasp of the style of writing, particularly the grammar and vocabulary used. Once you have a feel for this kind of writing continue Mark Miword's report of the Snow White court case using the above as your opening paragraph.

◆ Develop an improvisation of the scene outside the court room when Snow White emerges following the completion of the court case. You will need to decide who will be Snow White; the number of journalists representing various newspapers, radio stations and television stations; which station, program, or newspaper you represent; and who will be Ms Snow White's lawyer?

As in many real life situations outside court rooms, Ms Snow White may attempt to avoid some of your questions by answering 'no comment'. It is essential you have a range of questions worked out and that Ms Snow White and her lawyer have been given time before the improvisation to think about the questions they might be asked by journalists, and their replies.

◆ In groups of about five students organise the video taping of the improvisation. Each group should decide which news organisation they represent and then edit each video or audio tape as an item for that station's evening news program. Compare and contrast the presentations.

◆ Take one of the poems from this section and write a newspaper report for a major city daily newspaper about a court case that might have been conducted concerning the events set out in the poems.

◆ Choose another fairy tale and try to 'fracture' it by writing it from another perspective, just as D. J. Enright has done in **'The Other Version (1)'** and **'(2)'**.

Readers' Theatre

Snake

Voice 1 Look

    2 Shhh

    3 Don't make a noise

    1 Look at the snake

    2 Don't move

    3 If you move you die

 1,2,3 Shh . . .

    1 Move away very slowly

Brenton Mander
[British]

The Alphabet Speaks Up!

A   YOU

B   QUIET

C   HERE

D   LIGHTED TO MEET YOU

E   BY GUM

F   YOU LIKE

G   UP

H   OCOLATE

I   SPY

J   MES IS MY FRIEND

K   TE IS MY FRIEND TOO

L   NOT TELL YOU AGAIN

M   TALKING TO YOU

N   AND OUT

O   DEAR

P   NUTS

Q   HERE

R   YOU READY?

S   IT RAINING?

T   TIME

U   SMELL

V   RY NICE

W   DOUBLE ME

X   MARKS THE SPOT

Y   STOP NOW?

Z   WHO?

SAID ME!

David Horner
[British]

Waltzing Matilda

Carrying a Swag

Oh there once was a swagman camped in the billabongs,
    Under the shade of a Coolibah tree;
And he sang as he looked at the old billy boiling,
    "Who'll come a-waltzing Matilda with me."

    Who'll come a-waltzing Matilda, my darling,
        Who'll come a-waltzing Matilda with me.
    Waltzing Matilda and leading a water-bag,
        Who'll come a-waltzing Matilda with me.

Up came the jumbuck to drink at the waterhole,
    Up jumped the swagman and grabbed him in glee;
And he sang as he put him away in his tucker-bag,
    "You'll come a-waltzing Matilda with me."

    Who'll come a-waltzing Matilda, my darling,
        Who'll come a-waltzing Matilda with me.
    Waltzing Matilda and leading a water-bag,
        Who'll come a-waltzing Matilda with me.

Up came the squatter a-riding his thoroughbred;
    Up came policemen — one, two, and three.
"Whose is the jumbuck you've got in the tucker-bag?
    You'll come a-waltzing Matilda with we."

    Who'll come a-waltzing Matilda, my darling,
        Who'll come a-waltzing Matilda with me.
    Waltzing Matilda and leading a water-bag,
        Who'll come a-waltzing Matilda with me.

Up sprang the swagman and jumped in the waterhole,
    Drowning himself by the Coolibah tree;
And his voice can be heard as it sings in the billabongs,
    "Who'll come a-waltzing Matilda with me."

    Who'll come a-waltzing Matilda, my darling,
        Who'll come a-waltzing Matilda with me.
    Waltzing Matilda and leading a water-bag,
        Who'll come a-waltzing Matilda with me.

A. B. ('Banjo') Paterson
[Australian]

Leaves

Who's killed the leaves?
Me, says the apple. I've killed them all.
Fat as a bomb or a cannonball
I've killed the leaves.

Who sees them drop?
Me, says the pear, they will leave me all bare
So all the people can point and stare.
I see them drop.

Who'll catch their blood?
Me, me, me, says the marrow, the marrow.
I'll get so rotund that they'll need a wheelbarrow.
I'll catch their blood.

Who'll make their shroud?
Me, says the swallow, there's just time enough
Before I must pack all my spools and be off.
I'll make their shroud.

Who'll dig their grave?
Me, says the river, with the power of the clouds
A brown deep grave I'll dig under my floods.
I'll dig their grave.

Who'll be their parson?
Me, says the Crow, for it is well-known
I study the bible right down to the bone.
I'll be their parson.

Who'll be chief mourner?
Me, says the wind, I will cry through the glass
The people will pale and go cold when I pass.
I'll be chief mourner.

Who'll carry the coffin?
Me, says the sunset, the whole world will weep
To see me lower it into the deep.
I'll carry the coffin.

Who'll sing a psalm?
Me, says the tractor, with my gear grinding glottle
I'll plough up the stubble and sing through my throttle.
I'll sing the psalm.

Who'll toll the bell?
Me, says the robin, my song in October
Will tell the still gardens the leaves are over.
I'll toll the bell.

Ted Hughes
[British]

Cicadas

Afternoon, mid-August	
Two cicadas singing	Two cicadas singing
	Air kiln-hot, lead-heavy
Five cicadas humming	Five cicadas humming
Thunderhead northwestward	
Twelve cicadas buzzing	Twelve cicadas buzzing
	Up and down the street
the mighty choir's	the mighty choir's
assembling	assembling
Shrill cica-	
das	Ci-
droning	cadas
	droning
	in the elms
Three years	*Three years*
spent underground	
	among the roots
in darkness	in darkness
Now they're breaking ground	
	and climbing up
	the tree trunks
splitting skins	
and singing	and singing
	Jubilant
rejoicing	cicadas
	pouring out their
fervent praise	fervent praise
	for heat and light
their hymn	their hymn
sung to the sun	
Cicadas	Cicadas
	whining
whin-	
ing	ci-
	cadas
	whirring
whir-	
ring	ci-
	cadas
	pulsing
pulsing	
chanting from the treetops	chanting from the treetops
sending	
forth their	sending
booming	forth their
boisterous	booming
joyful noise!	joyful noise!

Paul Fleischman
[USA]

Notes

See the note on readers' theatre in the introduction to this anthology. **'Cicadas'**, a poem for two voices, requires practice, as words on the same line must be said in unison.

We have chosen to include **'Snake'** and **'The Alphabet Speaks Up!'** because they provide a convenient introduction to readers' theatre. **'Snake'** has the voices marked down the side of the poem and **'The Alphabet Speaks Up!'** has twenty-seven parts when each individual letter and the final line are spoken by different people. We hope that once you have experienced these two examples, you will feel confident about tackling the more difficult, yet well known, **'Waltzing Matilda'**.

Ted Hughes, the British Poet Laureate, has in **'Leaves'** taken a familiar nursery rhyme, *Who Killed Cock Robin*, and adapted it for his own purposes. He writes:

> In my poem, the leaves are the spirit of the living year. . . . [E]ach verse is part of a little fable, and each verse brings its fable to the story of the funeral of the leaves. At the same time, of course, each verse has to fit the real facts of autumn [in England].

One hundred years ago William Cawthorne adapted the rhyme for Australian children, *Who Killed Cock Robin?*, and his version was re-issued a few years ago, in a superbly illustrated picture book by Rodney McRae (1988, Margaret Hamilton, Sydney). Building on Cawthorne's first two stanzas, groups of students could produce their own Australian versions of this or another nursery rhyme. Here are the opening stanzas:

> Who killed Cockatoo?
> I, said the Morepork,
> With my tomahawk,
> I killed Cockatoo.
>
> Who saw him die?
> I, said the Possum,
> From the gum-blossom,
> I saw him die.
>
> *morepork*—variant of mopoke (an owl)

Activities

◆ Note that Cawthorne has followed closely the pattern of the original nursery rhyme, while Hughes has varied that pattern considerably. See if you can transform another nursery rhyme, such as *The House That Jack Built*, using the pattern for your own purpose.

Close Ups

The Face of the Horse

Animals do not sleep. At night
They stand over the world like a stone wall.

The cow's retreating head
Rustles the straw with its smooth horns,
The rocky brow a wedge
Between age-old cheek bones,
And the mute eyes
Turning sluggishly.

There's more intelligence and beauty in the horse's
    face.
He hears the talk of leaves and stones.
Intent, he knows the animal's cry
And the nightingale's murmur in the copse.

And knowing all, to whom may be recount
His wonderful visions?
The night is hushed. In the dark sky
Constellations rise.
The horse stands like a knight keeping watch.
The wind plays in his light hair,
His eyes burn like two huge worlds,
And his mane lifts like the imperial purple.

And if a man should see
The horse's magical face,
He would tear out his own impotent tongue
And give it to the horse. For
This magical creature is surely worthy of it.
Then we should hear words.
Words large as apples. Thick
As honey or butter-milk.

Words which penetrate like flame
And, once within the soul, like fire in some hut,
Illuminate its wretched trappings,
Words which do not die
And which we celebrate in song.

But now the stable is empty,
The trees have dispersed,
Pinch-faced morning has swaddled the hills,
Unlocked the fields for work.
And the horse, caged within its shafts,
Dragging a covered wagon,
Gazes out of its meek eyes
Upon the enigmatic, stationary world.

Nikolai Zabolotsky
(translated by Daniel Weissbort)
[Russian]

At Grass

The eye can hardly pick them out
From the cold shade they shelter in,
Till wind distresses tail and mane;
Then one crops grass, and moves about
— The other seeming to look on —
And stands anonymous again.

Yet fifteen years ago, perhaps
Two dozen distances sufficed
To fable them: faint afternoons
Of Cups and Stakes and Handicaps,
Whereby their names were artificed
To inlay faded, classic Junes —

Silks at the start: against the sky
Numbers and parasols: outside,
Squadrons of empty cars, and heat,
And littered grass: then the long cry
Hanging unhushed till it subside
To stop-press columns on the street.

Do memories plague their ears like flies?
They shake their heads. Dusk brims the shadows.
Summer by summer all stole away,
The starting-gates, the crowds and cries —
All but the unmolesting meadows.
Almanacked, their names live; they

Have slipped their names, and stand at ease,
Or gallop for what must be joy,
And not a fieldglass sees them home,
Or curious stop-watch prophesies:
Only the groom, and the groom's boy,
With bridles in the evening come.

Philip Larkin
[British]

The Horses

I climbed through woods in the hour-before-dawn dark.
Evil air, a frost-making stillness,

Not a leaf, not a bird, —
A world cast in frost. I came out above the wood

Where my breath left tortuous statues in the iron light.
But the valleys were draining the darkness

Till the moorline — blackening dregs of the brightening grey —
Halved the sky ahead. And I saw the horses:

Huge in the dense grey — ten together —
Megalith-still. They breathed, making no move,

With draped manes and tilted hind-hooves,
Making no sound.

I passed: not one snorted or jerked its head.
Grey silent fragments

Of grey silent world.

I listened in emptiness on the moor-ridge.
The curlew's tear turned its edge on the silence.

Slowly detail leafed from the darkness. Then the sun
Orange, red, red erupted

Silently, and splitting to its core tore and flung cloud,
Shook the gulf open, showed blue,

And the big planets hanging —
I turned

Stumbling in the fever of a dream, down towards
The dark woods, from the kindling tops,

And came to the horses.
                    There, still they stood.
But now steaming and glistening under the flow of light,

Their draped stone manes, their tilted hind-hooves
Stirring under a thaw while all around them

The frost showed its fires. But still they made no sound.
Not one snorted or stamped

Their hung heads patient as the horizons,
High over valleys, in the red levelling rays —

In din of the crowded streets, going among the years, the faces,
May I still meet my memory in so lonely a place

Between the streams and the red clouds, hearing curlews,
Hearing the horizons endure.

Ted Hughes
[British]

Horses at Grass

Ending their days at grass,
an indication of their prowess,
two gelded warriors of the turf
lift their heads and sniff as we
approach. Our escort calls them
Bill and Red; he doesn't know
the names that won them fame.
Legends grow from those that die
in harness; those who end their days
at grass, grow only fat.

The former Chairman of the Board
on his last official visit to
the office, gave me some Aster
seedlings he had raised. He snorted
when I thanked him; I took
them home for my nine-year-old
to plant in his very own garden.

      The chatterings of the typists
cease; I put aside the figurings
for the boss, the computations of
profit and loss. This is his whole
world, this is his end.

Leon Slade
[Australian]

Notes

Nikolai Zabolotsky was born in 1903 in Russia. His poem is particularly striking in its imagery.

Leon Slade is an Australian poet, born in Melbourne in 1931. **'Horses at Grass'** also pairs well with **'At Grass'**.

Activities

In Philip Larkin's **'At Grass'** and Ted Hughes's **'The Horses'** we have two poems by modern English poets that invite close comparison. In groups, discuss the following starter questions:

◆ What similarities do you find in the two poems? What differences?

◆ In **'At Grass'**, the word 'names' keeps recurring. What idea is being developed here? (It is broached in the first stanza by the use of 'anonymous'.)

◆ What is each poet's attitude to the horses?

Another Ted Hughes poem useful in this general context is 'A Dream of Horses'.

Reptilian Adventures

The Snake in the Department Store

Two farm boys riding bikes along a track
come rolling to a stop when up ahead
a ripple of the loose dirt seems to move.
They watch the brown snake cast a wavy tread

no wider than the lines their bike tyres make
and then instinctively they drop their bikes
together like a bingle, rush the snake
and pin his angry head down with a stick.

The body flings itself around as much
as what is pinning it keeps straight and still.
For several minutes, while a bike wheel spins,
these different four-foot lengths compete until

an end is plucked out of the movement
and the snake is hoisted into straining air.
Unsure of what to do with such a prize
the boy not holding it suggests a dare.

His day-pack is unzipped and emptied out,
then cautiously the snake is lowered in,
the stick is used again and soon withdrawn
and the zipper quickly given back its grin.

With motion going nowhere in their pack
the two boys pedal five miles into town,
debating how and where this slippery jack
might possibly be let out of his box.

The town is quiet on a Wednesday.
Outside the PATTERSON'S DEPARTMENT STORE
a ute is parked with a half a dozen sheep,
one fly-struck, wafting farm smells through the door.

The boys decide that this looks like the spot
for their experiment, and saunter in
to find themselves in FURNITURE. The squat
puffed shapes of bargain lounge suites crowd the room.

Two ladies dressed in floral patterns, both
of which would look at home on cushions, stand
examining a striped reclining chair.
One lady has a brochure in her hand.

The boys, pretending to be interested
in something nearby, set the day-pack on
a sofa, pull the zipper back enough
and wander over to an Aubusson-

style carpet crafted in the Philippines.
The snake comes oozing through the daylight slit
and disappears beneath the sofa's bulk.
Nothing happens for a while, then it

emerges from the other side and slides
behind the unobservant ladies, goes
between a pair of chairs and out of sight
again. It's gone. Then suddenly it flows

serenely down the aisle and through the door.
The boys arrive to see it cross behind
the man returning to his ute and pour
like dirty water after summer rain

into a gutter grate. They stand there on
the footpath while the man backs out his flock
and feel that since the snake was never seen
the whole affair has somehow been a flop.

Philip Hodgins
[Australian]

Snake

A narrow fellow in the grass
Occasionally rides.
You may have met him—did you not?
His notice sudden is.

The grass divides as with a comb,
A spotted shaft is seen,
And then it closes at your feet
And opens further on.

He likes a boggy acre,
A floor too cool for corn;
Yet when a boy and barefoot,
I more than once at noon

Have passed, I thought, a whiplash
Unbraiding in the sun;
When, stooping to secure it,
It wrinkled and was gone.

Several of nature's people
I know, and they know me;
I feel for them a transport
Of cordiality,

But never met this fellow,
Attended or alone,
Without a tighter breathing
And zero at the bone.

Emily Dickinson
[USA]

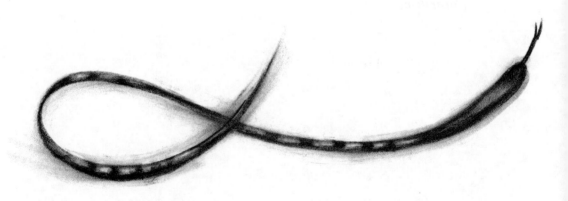

Forever the Snake

Awkward on a hillock of grass
feet falling forward over the edge
cramped close to the children
away from the snake.

And in that patch of long reed it is waiting.

You pick up a spade.
Eyes pace out the ground.
Your left hand is clenched on itself
nails bite into your skin.

A heavy grey rock lies in the reeds.
With one move you upend it.
The children edge closer on the hilly rise
they stand on my feet.

I see you consider and bend
you probe with the spade.

And then it is here.

Snake. Flashing its back
arrowing through grass
black missile with small guiding head
firing off reflexes, straight into attack.

And the spade. Lifeless and foreign
under your hand raised in the air.

This black speeding nerve is cutting through space.

Somewhere forever your hand is raised
in far-off space fields the snake is racing.

Now the thick spade crashes down from above
snapping the nerve that even in death sends its messages.

We inch about on our hillock of earth.
The back of the snake is still thrashing.
You stand with its head under your spade
you are locked to its spine.

Far-out in space the snake is still speeding
rushing through grass to attack.

Closer in space the spade has been raised.

Here on the grass the black nerve is broken.

Yet always the snake is now striking
in the quiet, in the space beyond time.

Jennifer Rankin
[Australian]

Notes

All three poets in this section draw on powerful metaphors to express the movement, shape and behaviour of snakes. The story that Hodgins tells is full of life and energy and captures beautifully the 'experiment' the boys manage to pull off; an experiment which ends up seeming 'a flop'. **'Snake (A narrow fellow in the grass)'** and **'Forever the Snake'** written on different continents, both capture the fear that the appearance of a snake can induce. The variation in line length and the punctuation of Rankin's poem needs careful examination.

Emily Dickinson (1830–86) was a US poet who composed over 1000 lyrics before her early death. She wrote in secret and published nothing during her lifetime.

Jennifer Rankin (1941–79) an Australian writer and poet was published widely before her early death.

Activities

◆ Make a list of all the metaphors used to describe the snake in the three poems.

◆ Make a list of other metaphors you might use to describe a snake.

◆ Do you have a favourite snake story? Using Philip Hodgins' poem as a model, write a narrative poem which imaginatively tells a 'tall story' about an adventure with a snake.

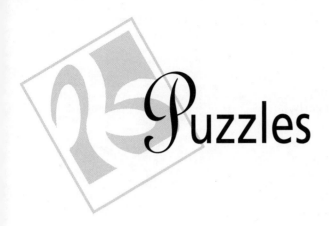

25 $\mathcal{P}$uzzles

Riddle

I am something
that has been changed

Once I was green and springy
Then I was brown and tough
Next I was red and brittle
At last I am soft and grey

I am so light
one snowflake does not rest
so gently upon another

so gentle that one
downy feather is not so light
against another
on a pigeon's breast

I have been changed indeed
and now I am finished

Once green and lively
I have been made use of
and now they treat me like dirt

a light grey slight soft and falling thing
yet if you weighed me in the balance
you would find me of more weight
than that from which I was made

Who am I then?
Tell me quick
before I am brushed away

John Birtwhistle
[British]

Riddles

1
Mermaids' tears, crusted with time,
Wept long ago, now gather them early,
Trailing beards and trailing slime,
Little morsels, salt and pearly.

2
Made of nothing, but not cheap,
Leave me alone: I break, my dear.
Made for a friend, but yours to keep,
And if you keep me I disappear.

3
Yellow fingers, rooted in earth
Beneath the moon, where moths flutter,
Pull them to their monstrous birth
And boil them in a dish with butter.

John Fuller
[British]

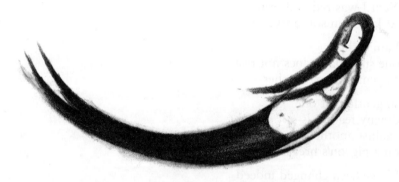

Snake Riddle

Why didn't the viper
Vipe 'er nose?
Because the adder
'ad 'er 'andkerchief.

Anon.

Parable I

The doors were golden, studded with jewels,
Foliate scroll-work that twisted and curled.
There were carved stories of love, hate, duels,
A lady's trial, and a hero's return.

People gathered in the marble porch,
Showed off their fashions, talked with friends,
Glanced briefly at the carvings on the doors,
Then borrowed some money or sold some bread.

The porch became a market place
With roughly erected booths and stalls.
Travellers bought local trinkets and cakes,
Stared for a while, till the sculpture palled.

Experts on art peered at the doors,
Wrote volumes about each well-moulded inch.
Officials muttered, 'Is it insured?'
And fitted the porch with litter bins.

But in all the centuries people came,
To see or be seen, buy cakes or write,
No one has yet, to this very day,
Unfastened the doors and stepped inside.

Leo Aylen
[British]

Notes

John Birtwhistle, an English poet, has another poem, **'The Hitch-hiker's Curse on Being Passed By'**, on page 86. John Fuller, another English poet, has several volumes of verse, including *Squeaking Crust* (Chatto and Windus) from which these riddles are taken. (The title poem in *Squeaking Crust* is excellent for oral presentation.)

Activities

◆ Work in small groups to solve each riddle, then the class can further explore the whole design of the poems. (Answers to riddles are on p. 161.)

Ballads and Stories

The Streets of Laredo

As I walked out in the streets of Laredo.
As I walked out in Laredo one day,
I spied a young cowboy all wrapped in white linen,
All wrapped in white linen as cold as the clay.

'I see by your outfit that you are a cowboy'—
These words he did say as I boldly stepped by.
'Come sit down beside me and hear my sad story:
I'm shot in the breast and I know I must die.

'It was once in the saddle I used to go dashing,
Once in the saddle I used to go gay;
First to the ale-house and then to the jail-house,
Got shot in the breast and I'm dying today.

'Get six jolly cowboys to carry my coffin;
Get six pretty maidens to carry my pall;
Put bunches of roses all over my coffin,
Roses to deaden the clods as they fall.

'Oh, beat the drum slowly and play the fife lowly,
Play the dead march as you carry me along:
Take me to the green valley and lay the sod o'er me,
For I'm a young cowboy and I know I've done wrong.

'Go gather around you a crowd of young cowboys
And tell them the story of this, my sad fate;
Tell one and the other before they go further
To stop their wild roving before it's too late.

'Go fetch me a cup, a cup of cold water
To cool my parched lips,' the cowboy then said.
Before I returned, the spirit had left him
And gone to its Maker—the cowboy was dead.

We beat the drum slowly and played the fife lowly,
And bitterly wept as we carried him along;
For we all loved our comrade, so brave, young and handsome,
We all loved our comrade although he'd done wrong.

Anon.

Ballad

A knight went down to the river's rim
And saw a nymph glance back at him.

'The river's daughter herself I am,'
And into his waiting arms she swam.

Then summer's ardour stretched out and loved
As the cool water beneath him moved.

But when their loving force was spent
The nymph dissolved in her element.

And after many great vows and tall
The knight rode away by the steep cliff wall.

'I'll come this way again,' he said,
'And marry the nymph of the river bed.'

The knight rode away and remembered his cares;
'First I must settle my weighty affairs,

Instruct the steward of my estate,
And fix the bolt on the garden gate;

Must pay my men and harvest the grain
Before I come back to the river again.'

The gate is fixed, the grain is sold,
The weather grows bleak, the year turns cold,

And part of the river is frozen over
As the nymph awaits the return of her lover.

The knight is having a Christmas fling
And tells his heart it has time until spring.

He dances with his neighbour's daughter,
Who's as gold to silver, as sun to water.

So he forgets the song of the river
And swears new love for ever and ever.

Now handsome knight and lovely bride
In the month of May to the river ride

Together with many guests of rank
They ride along to the river-bank.

And down the hill clip-clops their train
Who will not return that way again.

'My bride, my bride, why do we go
To where the sullen waters flow?'

But the bride shines blond as the midday sun
But she and the knight and the guests are undone.

They ride past the cliff where the waters moan
And are turned forever to rocks and stone.

Cold as rock and as still and stiff
They now form part of the river's cliff:

The guests on horseback, the monk, the bride
And the faithless bridegroom at her side.

But the nymph looks up and repents her deed:
'I should have allowed them to pass,' she said,

'For turned to stone, forever they'll be
A sorrow and a reproach to me.'

The centuries pass, the pleasure-boats go
Carrying sightseers to and fro

Who in their time will turn as stiff:
For all, all is water beneath the cliff.

Gerda Mayer
[British]

Unidentified Flying Object

It's true Mattie Lee
has clean disappeared.
And shouldn't we notify
the sheriff? No use, Will
insists, no earthly use.

He was sleeping one off
under the trees that night,
he claims, and woke up when
the space-ship
landed—a silvery dome

with grassy-green and red-
hot-looking lights like eyes
that stared blinked stared.
Says he hid himself
in the bushes and watched,

shaking. Pretty soon
a hatch slides open, a ramp
glides forward like
a glowing tongue poked out.
And who or what is it

silently present there?
Same as if Will's
trying to peer through webs
and bars of gauzy glare
screening, distorting a shape

he sees yet cannot see.
But crazier than that
was when Mattie Lee
came running from her house
towards the thing.

She's wearing her sunflower hat
and the dress the lady she cooked
for gave her, and it's like
she's late for work the way
she scurries up the ramp.

And it seems to Will
that in its queer
shining, plain Mattie Lee's
transformed—is every teasing brown
he'd ever wanted, never had.

He's fixing to shout, Come back,
Mattie Lee, come back;
but a heavy hand is over his mouth
when he hears her laugh
as she steps inside.

without even a goodbye glance
around. The next Will knew,
the UFO rose in the air—
no blastoff roar, no flame,
he says—hung in the dark,

hovered, shimmered,
its eyes pulsing, then whirred
spiraling into the sky,
vanished as though
it had never been.

Will's tale anyhow.
All I'm certain of
is Mattie Lee's
nowhere to be found
and must have gone

off in a hurry. Left her doors
unlocked and the radio on
and a roast in the oven. Strange.
As for Will, he's a changed man,
not drinking nowadays and sad.

Mattie Lee's friends—
she's got no kinfolks, lived
alone—are worried, swear
Will was craving her
and she held herself too good

for him, being head of Mount
Nebo's usher board and such.
And some are hinting what I,
for one—well, never mind.
The talk is getting mean.

Robert Hayden
[USA]

Faces in the Street

They lie, the men who tell us in a loud decisive tone
That want is here a stranger, and that misery's unknown;
For where the nearest suburb and the city proper meet
My window-sill is level with the faces in the street—
      Drifting past, drifting past,
      To the beat of weary feet—
While I sorrow for the owners of those faces in the street.

And cause I have to sorrow, in a land so young and fair,
To see upon those faces stamped the marks of Want and Care;
I look in vain for traces of the fresh and fair and sweet
In sallow, sunken faces that are drifting through the street—
      Drifting on, drifting on,
      To the scrape of restless feet;
I can sorrow for the owners of the faces in the street.

In hours before the dawning dims the starlight in the sky
The wan and weary faces first begin to trickle by,
Increasing as the moments hurry on with morning feet,
Till like a pallid river flow the faces in the street—
      Flowing in, flowing in,
      To the beat of hurried feet—
Ah! I sorrow for the owners of those faces in the street.

The human river dwindles when 'tis past the hour of eight,
Its waves go flowing faster in the fear of being late;
But slowly drag the moments, whilst beneath the dust and heat
The city grinds the owners of the faces in the street—
      Grinding body, grinding soul,
      Yielding scarce enough to eat—
Oh! I sorrow for the owners of the faces in the street.

And then the only faces till the sun is sinking down
Are those of outside toilers and the idlers of the town,
Save here and there a face that seems a stranger in the street
Tells of the city's unemployed upon his weary beat—
      Drifting round, drifting round,
      To the tread of listless feet—
Ah! My heart aches for the owner of that sad face in the street.

And when the hours on lagging feet have slowly dragged away,
And sickly yellow gaslights rise to mock the going day,
Then flowing past my window like a tide in its retreat,
Again I see the pallid stream of faces in the street—
    Ebbing out, ebbing out,
    To the drag of tired feet,
While my heart is aching dumbly for the faces in the street.

And now all blurred and smirched with vice the day's sad pages end,
For while the short 'large hours' towards the longer 'small hours' trend,
With smiles that mock the wearer, and with words that half entreat,
Delilah pleads for custom at the corner of the street—
        Sinking down, sinking down,
        Battered wreck by tempests beat—
A dreadful, thankless trade is hers, that Woman of the Street.

But, ah! to dreader things than these our fair young city comes,
For in its heart are growing thick the filthy dens and slums,
Where human forms shall rot away in sties for swine unmeet,
And ghostly faces shall be seen unfit for any street—
        Rotting out, rotting out,
        For the lack of air and meat—
In dens of vice and horror that are hidden from the street.

I wonder would the apathy of wealthy men endure
Were all their windows level with the faces of the Poor?
Ah! Mammon's slaves, your knees shall knock, your hearts in terror beat,
When God demands a reason for the sorrows of the street,
        The wrong things and the bad things
        And the sad things that we meet
In the filthy lane and alley, and the cruel, heartless street.

I left the dreadful corner where the steps are never still,
And sought another window overlooking gorge and hill;
But when the night came dreary with the driving rain and sleet,
They haunted me—the shadows of those faces in the street,
        Flitting by, flitting by,
        Flitting by with noiseless feet,
And with cheeks but little paler than the real ones in the street.

Once I cried: 'O God Almighty! if Thy might doth still endure,
Now show me in a vision for the wrongs of Earth a cure.'
And, lo! with shops all shuttered I beheld a city's street,
And in the warning distance heard the tramp of many feet,
        Coming near, coming near,
        To a drum's dull distant beat,
And soon I saw the army that was marching down the street.

Then, like a swollen river that has broken bank and wall,
The human flood came pouring with the red flags over all,
And kindled eyes all blazing bright with revolutions's heat,
And flashing swords reflecting rigid faces in the street.
        Pouring on, pouring on,
        To a drum's loud threatening beat,
And the war-hymns and the cheering of the people in the street.

And so it must be while the world goes rolling round its course,
The warning pen shall write in vain, the warning voice grow hoarse,
But not until a city feels Red Revolution's feet
Shall its sad people miss awhile the terrors of the street —
      The dreadful everlasting strife
      For scarcely clothes and meat
In that pent track of living death — the city's cruel street.

Henry Lawson
[Australian]

What has Happened to Lulu?

What has happened to Lulu, mother?
    What has happened to Lu?
There's nothing in her bed but an old rag doll
    And by its side a shoe.

Why is her window wide, mother,
    The curtain flapping free,
And only a circle on the dusty shelf
    Where her money-box used to be?

Why do you turn your head, mother,
    And why do the tear-drops fall?
And why do you crumple that note on the fire
    And say it is nothing at all?

I woke to voices late last night,
    I heard an engine roar.
Why do you tell me the things I heard
    Were a dream and nothing more?

I heard somebody cry, mother,
    In anger or in pain,
But now I ask you why, mother,
    You say it was a gust of rain.

Why do you wander about as though
    You don't know what to do?
What has happened to Lulu, mother?
    What has happened to Lu?

Charles Causley
[British]

Song

King Julius left the south country
His banners all bravely flying;
His followers went out with Jubilee
But they shall return with sighing.

Loud arose the triumphal hymn
The drums were loudly rolling,
Yet you might have heard in distance dim
How a passing bell was tolling.

The sword so bright from battles won
With unseen rust is fretting,
The evening comes before the noon,
The scarce risen sun is setting.

While princes hang upon his breath
And nations round are fearing,
Close by his side a daggered death
With sheathless point stands sneering.

That death he took a certain aim,
For Death is stony-hearted
And in the zenith of his fame
Both power and life departed.

Emily Brontë
[British]

 # Notes

There is no shortage of material on ballads. Famous ballads include: Scott's *Lochinvar*, Coleridge's *The Ryme of the Ancient Mariner* and Kipling's *Ballad of East and West*.

Nancy Keesing and Douglas Stewart published a large collection in their *Australian Bush Ballads*. There is great energy in much of this verse.

Charles Causley, the Cornish poet, is one of the few modern poets (W. H. Auden is another) who regularly make use of the traditional ballad metre (a four-lined stanza with four beats to the first and third lines, and three in the second and fourth, and with the second and fourth lines rhyming). He has described **'What Has Happened to Lulu?'** as 'a kind of detective story' without a given solution.

'Song' is very different to the ballads in this section. Emily Brontë tells a story and wittily makes a moral point.

 # Activities

◆ In small groups discuss the poem **'What Has Happened to Lulu?'** to provide a solution to the title's question, using the clues provided in the poem. There are many possible explanations. Note that all the stanzas except the penultimate (second last) one pose questions. In this respect, the poem is similar to one of the most famous of all the old ballads, *Edward, Edward* (which varies the form somewhat).

◆ Try writing a ballad which asks a series of questions. Ballad metre is perhaps the easiest to imitate, and is a good form to try once you have gained confidence in writing free-verse.

◆ Seek out some of the old ballads and present them to the class as readers' theatre. All the following tell a story simply and powerfully and are readily available in anthologies: *The Unquiet Grave*, *The Wife of Usher's Well*, *Lord Randal*, *The Golden Vanity* and *Sir Patrick Spens*.

Perspectives

Stars

(for Emma, on her first birthday)

I cannot count the times
I nearly woke you
to show you stars
to trace constellations
to whisper their names to you
because I want you
to learn of things that last.
Even now.
Even as you begin to walk
away from me.

Paul B. Janeczko
[USA]

Assessment

While I was a young man, Time was old.
He shuffled along wherever he went.
His rags were the colors of rotting apples.
He paid no attention to me.

Now Time is young and fast and muscular.
He wears his ball cap backward.
He races past me on his roller-blades,
gracefully turns on a toe and comes back.

Ted Kooser
[USA]

A Consumer's Report

The name of the product I tested is *Life*,
I have completed the form you sent me
and understand that my answers are confidential.

I had it as a gift,
I didn't feel much while using it,
in fact I think I'd have liked to be more excited.
It seemed gentle on the hands
but left an embarrassing deposit behind.
It was not economical
and I have used much more than I thought
(I suppose I have about half left
but it's difficult to tell) —
although the instructions are fairly large
there are so many of them
I don't know which to follow, especially
as they seem to contradict each other.
I'm not sure such a thing
should be put in the way of children —
It's difficult to think of a purpose
for it. One of my friends says
it's just to keep its maker in a job.
Also the price is much too high.
Things are piling up so fast,
after all, the world got by
for a thousand million years
without this, do we need it now?
(Incidentally, please ask your man
to stop calling me 'the respondent',
I don't like the sound of it.)
There seems to be a lot of different labels,
sizes and colours should be uniform,
the shape is awkward, it's waterproof
but not heat resistant, it doesn't keep
yet it's very difficult to get rid of:
whenever they make it cheaper they seem
to put less in — if you say you don't
want it, then it's delivered anyway.
I'd agree it's a popular product,
it's got into the language; people
even say they're on the side of it.
Personally I think it's overdone,
a small thing people are ready
to behave badly about. I think

we should take it for granted. If its
experts are called philosophers or market
researchers or historians, we shouldn't
care. We are the consumers and the last
law makers. So finally, I'd buy it.
But the question of a 'best buy'
I'd like to leave until I get
the competitive product you said you'd send.

Peter Porter
[Australian]

When

Death doesn't
end life
death just
interrupts it

a bookmark between page 256 and 257
a dental appointment of Friday at two
guests tonight
a movie tomorrow evening
a discussion that didn't end
coffee percolating on the stove
six shirts at the laundry
a holiday in Mexico this winter

this is what things are like
when a period is placed
in the middle of a sentence

Robert Zend
[Hungarian]

Bury Me

Bury me in a lotus pond
So that the eels may swish by my ears,
While on the lanterns — the green lotus leaves,
Fireflies flicker, now dim, now bright.

Bury me under the acacia flowers
So I may have sweet dreams forever;
Or bury me on top of Mount T'ai
Where the wind wails over a lone pine.
Or burn me to ashes and scatter me
In a river where spring tides are surging high,
So I may drift away with fallen petals
To a land that nobody knows.

Chu Hsiang
[Chinese]　　　*(translated by Kai-Yu Hsu)*

Notes

'Assessment'
ball cap—a baseball cap

Activities

◆ The structure of **'When'** is worth examining closely. The first stanza states the theme, the second consists of a series of images supporting the initial statement, and the third restates the theme. Since the poem has been translated into Canadian English, the word 'period' has been used where we would use 'full stop'. Would anything be gained, or lost, if 'full stop' were substituted for period?

◆ In groups, consider the tone of each of these poems about death. They could also be used as the starting point for a discussion of humankind's quest to prolong life and the desire of some for immortality. A link could be made with the Struldbrugs in Book III of Swift's *Gulliver's Travels*.

◆ **'A Consumer's Report'** should be read aloud following preparation—experiment with different voices, and be sure to vary the pace and intonation where appropriate.

◆ After discussing Peter Porter's clever poem, students might like to imagine the 'competitive product' and describe it in similar terms, or design posters for *Life* incorporating typical advertising appeals.

◆ Make a list of the 'commercial' jargon and phrases used by Porter.

The answers to the riddles posed in the poems are:

    'Riddle' (John Birtwhistle)—wood ash

    'Three Riddles' (John Fuller)—oysters; a promise; parsnips (or carrots).

Index of Titles and First Lines

A boy bowls up on the edge of the red sand.   109

A Consumer's Report   158

A Day Too Late   56

A fruit bat skims along the lights.   42

A knight went down to the river's rim   148

A narrow fellow in the grass   140

A YOU   128

Afternoon, mid-August   131

Although you have given me a stomach upset,   54

Among twenty snowy mountains,   23

Animals do not sleep. At night   133

Around the High School   67

As I walked out in the streets of Laredo.   147

Ash Wednesday   45

Assessment   157

At Grass   134

Awkward on a hillock of grass   141

Ballad   148

Beneath the trees   68

Bran Nue Day   97

Breakers   44

Bury me in a lotus pond   160

Bury Me   160

'Bye dear no, I won't drive fast.   87

canter canter canter canter   85

Car Salesman   31

Catching Crabs   92

Cicadas   131

Columbus from his after-   90

Come Live With Me and be My Girl   62

Come live with me, and be my love,   60

Conform to safety standards, have been rigorously checked,   6

Consumer Poems   6

Dear Sir,   37

Death doesn't   159

Dinner at my Sister's   58

Discovered an old rocking-horse in Woolworth's,   119

Drop Kick   12

Ending their days at grass   136

Every Child's Book of Animal Stories.   71

Every morning they hold hands   58

Examiner   73

Faces in the Street   173

First Fight   16

First paint a cage   109

First, I saw her feet   119

For Grannie Coolwell   98

Forever the Snake   141

Fourteen Ways of Touching the Peter   27

Framed in his showroom, tinted and furbished well   31

From out of the spirit world   100

from *The Cantbeworried Tales*   32

from *The Canterbury Tales*   32

from *The Emigrants*   90

Gentle hunter   105

'Ghost Wanted; Young, Willing'   37

Giorgio de Chirico   111

He squats beside an antique sewing-machine   34

He thrust his joy against the weight of the sea   16

He's on your hammer, closing in with every bounce   12

Heaving mountain in the sea,   43

Homophones   82

Horses at Grass   136

How many sentences wander each day
   9

How to Paint the Portrait of a Bird
   109

I am something   143

I cannot count the times   157

I climbed through the woods in the
   hour-before-dawn dark.   135

I don't know what it is,   53

I dwell on the misty steppe   104

I had a silver penny   123

I sat all morning in the college sick bay
   77

I will give my love an apple without
   e'er a core   50

I will give my love an apple without
   e'er a core,   50

If all the world and love were young,
   61

If the world is going to end   45

If you'll give me a kiss and be my girl
   62

Immigrants at Central Station, 1951
   95

Impossible black   94

Into the Landscape   42

Is it like a carnival with spangles and
   balloons,   49

It had no radio   76

It is always late afternoon   111

It is midnight.   7

It was sad to hear   95

It's Raining in Love   53

It's true Mattie Lee   150

Junior Coaching   14

King Julius left the south country   155

Last night a pair of eyes   46

Leaves   130

Leopard   105

Listen   67

Living Language   9

Love   49

Love's Coming   56

Man Lying on a Wall   111

Masons, when they start upon a
   building,   53

Mermaids' tears, crusted with time,
   144

Mid-term Break   77

Migrant Woman on a Melbourne Tram
   94

Mimi Dancers   100

My mind has thunderstorms,   9

New Moon   106

"Nitgub," said the typewriter,   83

Not Enough Dough? Tough!   80

nothing depends   29

Novel Lesson   68

Now the new Moon is hanging, having
   cast away his bone: 106

Nursery Rhyme of Innocence and
   Experience   123

O how I love you baby,   52

Oh there once was a swagman camped
   in the billabongs,   129

Once upon a valley   118

Orgy   85

Our Freda had a nasty experience the
   other night.   121

Out in the Golfe de Gascogne, on the
   far   15

Parable I   145

Paring the Apple   112

Passengers to the City   57

Pencil   8

Perfect Beggar   34

Pine Tree   44

Place Kick   13

POLICE ARE SEEKING TO
   IDENTIFY THE PILLION RIDER
   WHO WAS ALSO KILLED   59

Prize-Giving   50

Professor Eisenbart, asked to attend
   50

Quietly as rosebuds   56

Riddle   143
Riddles   144
Ruby and me stalking savannah   92
Scaffolding   53
Simply Being Jim   35
Sleeping Snow White   121
Snake Riddle   144
Snake   127
Snake   140
Snap Shot   12
Snapshots   5
so much depends   29
Someone writes with me   8
Song   155
Stars   157
Still somewhere in the rule-book   13
Stop All the Clocks   55
Stop all the clocks, cut off the
   telephone,   55
Suburban Lovers   58
Summary of a Western   117
Sunlight pillars through glass, probes
   each desk   68
Symptoms   54
tennis shoe,   69
The 'word' of an antelope caught in a
   trap   104
The Alphabet Speaks Up!   128
The Angry Man   34
The Anguish of The Machine   84
The birds saw the people walking
   along.   105
The birds   105
The butchers laid waste the islands
   93
The Cricketers   109
The Curlew Cried   101
The Curse of Your Wheels to you!   86
The doors were golden, studded with
   jewels,   145
The Evening Star   106
The Examination   74
The eye can hardly pick them out   134
The Face of the Horse   133

The Green Rambler   76
THE HEAT IS ON TOO MUCH
   PRESSURE PACKING UP   84
The Hitch-Hiker's Curse on Being
   Passed by   86
The Horse That Had a Flat Tire   118
The Horses   135
The Meaning   46
The Millere was a stout carl for the
   nones;   32
The name of the product I tested is
   Life,   158
The nimphs reply to the Sheepheard
   61
The noblest Kick that ever left a boot.
   12
The other day I chanced to meet   34
The Other Version (1)   121
The Other Version (2)   122
The Passionate Sheepheard to his love
   60
The Play Way   68
The Poem William Carlos Williams
   Never Wrote But Might Have, Had
   He Lived on Mangoes for a Year
   29
The Pop Star's Song   52
The Red Wheelbarrow   29
The routine trickery of the examination
   73
The Snake in the Department Store
   138
The Song of the Whale   43
The Spelling Prize   71
The Streets of Laredo   147
The Surfer   16
The Surf-Rider   15
The Television Poem   7
The Waiting Wolf   119
The waste from the chemical factory's
   stacks   42
The Winter Pond   41
The winter pond   41
There are portraits and still-lifes.   112

There must have been a girl once   121

These lapdogs of the sea   44

They are stones   6

They Come for the Islands (1493)   93

They lie, the men who tell us in a loud decisive tone   152

Thirteen Ways of Looking at a Blackbird   23

This fella song   97

This girl   70

This morning she is travelling   57

Three nights they heard the curlew cry.   101

Throughout those meals the slaughtering went on.   58

Thrown the ball up. Try to whack it   14

Thunderstorms   9

To Let Her Think Shadows   70

To The Station   87

Toast her, all, in parsnip wine,   80

Tonight, then, is the night;   16

Two farm boys riding along a track   138

Typo   83

Unholy Marriage   59

Unidentified Flying Object   150

Up and up soars the Evening Star, hanging there in the sky.   106

Voice 1 Look   127

Waltzing Matilda   129

Warning   36

We Are Going   98

'Well doctor, what do you think?'   74

We see a dusty desert scene and that's   117

What has Happened to Lulu?   154

What's in a Locker?   69

Whatever's the matter with Melanie?   75

Whatever's the matter with Melanie?   75

When I am an old woman I shall wear purple   36

When the planners breached at last   44

When you land in the bush   35

When   159

While I was a young man, Time was old.   157

Whitefellas are rich   99

Whitefellas   99

Who's killed the leaves?   130

Why didn't the viper   144

Winter Afternoon   42

Wood you believe that I didn't no   82

Words   6

You can push   27

You could draw a straight line from the heels,   111

You meet a man. You're looking for a hero,

You want the true story? Very well.   233

You'd Better Believe Him — A Fable   119

Index of Poets

Adamson, Robert (Australian) 42

Ai Ching (Chinese) 41

Arnhem land, indigenous people (Australian) 105

Auden, W. H. (British) 55

Aylen, Leo (British) 62, 145

Birtwhistle, John (British) 86, 143

Boothroyd, J. R. (British) 87

Brathwaite, Edward (Barbadian) 90

Brautigan, Richard (United States) 53, 118

Breen, B. A. (Australian) 70

Brontë, Emily (British) 155

Causley, Charles (British) 123, 154

Chaucer, Geoffrey (English) 32

Chu Hsiang (Chinese) 160

Chi, Jimmy (Australian) 97

Coon, George E. (United States) 82

Dabydeen, David (Guyanan) 92

Davies, W. H. (British) 9

Dawe, Bruce (Australian) 37, 58

DePauw, Dennis (United States) 76

Dickinson, Emily (United States) 140

Donald, Jane (Australian) 9

Enright, D. J. (British) 121

Fisher, Catherine (British) 6

Fleischman, Paul (United States) 131

Fuller, John (British) 144

Gallagher, Katherine (Australian) 57

Ghose, Zulfikar (Pakistan) 15

Gill, David (British) 34

Gillilan, Pamela (British) 121

Guess, Jeff (Australian) 68, 109

Hannah, Sophie (British) 54, 56, 117

Haraway, Fran (United States) 69

Harry, J. S. (Australian) 42

Harwood, Gwen (Australian) 50, 71

Hayden, Robert (United States) 150

Heaney, Seamus (Irish) 53, 68, 77

Hoban, Russell (United States) 83

Hodgins, Philip (Australian) 12, 13, 46, 111, 138

Holbrook, David (British) 59

Horner, David (British) 128

Hughes, Ted (British) 130, 135

Janeczko, Paul B. (United States) 157

Joseph, Jenny (British) 36

Kooser, Ted (United States) 157

Larkin, Philip (British) 134

Laue, John (United States) 67

Lawson, Henry (Australian) 152

Longley, Michael (British) 111

Lowbury, Edward (British) 44

MacBeth, George (British) 27

Macfarlane, Peter (Australian) 45

McGinley, Phyllis (United States) 34

McGough, Roger (British) 74

Mafi-Williams, Lorraine (Australian) 100

Mander, Brenton (British) 127

Manolis, Mick (Australian) 97

Marlowe, Christopher (English) 60

Mayer, Gerda (British) 148

Morgan, Edwin (British) 85

Morgan, Pete (British) 7

Murphy, Peter (British) 84

Neruda, Pablo (Chilean) 93

Oodgeroo Noonuccal (Australian) 98, 101

Page, Geoff (Australian) 44

Palmateer, R. (United States) 29

Paterson, A. B. ('Banjo') (Australian) 129

Patten, Brian (British) 119

Porter, Peter (Australian)   158
Post-Primary Boys' Class Papunya
    School Papunya Settlement
    (Australian)   99
Prévert, Jacques (French)   110
Raleigh, Sir Walter (English)   61
Random, William (British)   80
Rankin, Jennifer (Australian)   141
Redgrove, Peter (British)   25
Sail, Lawrence (British)   6
Sandag (Mongolian)   104
Saw, Ian (Australian)   35
Scammell, William (British)   14
Scannell, Vernon (British)   16, 49, 52
Scott, F. R. (British)   73
Skrzynecki, Peter (Australian)   95

Slade, Leon (Australian)   136
Stevens, Wallace (United States)   23
Strauss, Gwen (United States)   119
Strauss, Jennifer (Australian)   94
Swain, David (Australian)   32
Thiele, Colin (Australian)   31
Tomlinson, Charles (British)   112
Toriba poetry (Nigerian)   105
Wade, Barry (British)   75
Williams, William Carlos (United
    States)   29
Wright, Judith (Australian)   16
Wright, Kit (British)   43
Zabolotsky, Nikolai (Russian)   133
Zend, Robert (Hungarian)   8, 159

Acknowledgments

The authors and publishers wish to thank copyright holders for granting permission to reproduce poems and paintings. Sources are as follows:

W. H. Auden: 'Stop all the clocks, cut off the telephone', 'Twelve Songs', from *Collected Poems*, Faber and Faber Ltd; Leo Aylen: 'Parable 1', 'Come Live with Me and Be My Girl', from *Sunflower*, Sidgwick & Jackson Ltd; John Birtwhistle: 'The Hitch-hikers Curse on Being Passed By', 'Riddle', Anvil Poetry; Edward Kamau Brathwaite: 'The Emigrants', from *The Arrivants* by Edward Kamau Brathwaite (1973), by permission of Oxford University Press, Oxford; Richard Brautigan: 'It's Raining in Love', from *The Pill Versus the Springhill Mine Disaster*, Delacorte Press, 1968; B. A. Breen: 'To Let Her Think Shadows', from *Behind My Eyes*, by permission of the author; Charles Causley: 'Nursery Rhyme of Innocence and Experience', 'What Has Happened to Lulu', from *Collected Poems*, Macmillan Publishers Ltd; Jimmy Chi & Mick Manolis: 'Bran Nue Day', from *Bran Nue Dae* by Jimmy Chi & Kuckles, Magabala Books/Currency Press, 1991, reprinted by permission of Bran Nue Dae Productions; George E. Coon: 'Homophones', from *The Reading Teacher*, by permission of the author and International Reading Association; W. H. Davies: 'Thunderstorms', reprinted by permission of the Estate of W. H. Davies; Bruce Dawe: 'Suburban Lovers', 'Dinner at My Sister's', 'Ghost Wanted: Young Willing', from *Sometime Gladness Collected Poems 1954-1992*, Addison Wesley Longman; Dennis DePauw: 'The Green Rambler', Lincoln High School, Los Angeles; D. J. Enright: 'The Other Version (1)', 'The Other Version (2)', from *Rhyme Time Rhyme*, Watson, Little Limited; Paul Fleischman: 'Cicadas', from *Joyful Noise: Poems For Two Voices*, HarperCollins Publishers; John Fuller: 'Riddles', by permission of the author; Katherine Gallagher: 'Passenger to the City', Hale & Iremonger; Zulfikar Ghose: 'The Surf-Rider', from *Jets from Orange*, Macmillan Publishers Ltd; David Gill: 'Perfect Beggar', from *Men Without Evenings*, by permission of the author and Chatto & Windus; Pamela Gillilan: 'Sleeping Snow-White', by permission of the author; Jeff Guess: 'The Novel Lesson', first published in *South Australian Teachers Journal*, 'The Cricketers', first published in *Poetry Australia*, reprinted by permission of the author; Sophie Hannah: 'Symptoms', 'Day Too Late', 'Summary', from *Hero and the Girl Next Door*, Carcanet Press Limited; Fran Haraway: 'What's in a Locker?', reprinted by permission of the author; J. S. Harry: 'Into the Landscape', from *The Deer Under the Skin*, University of Queensland Press, reprinted by permission of the author; Gwen Harwood: 'Prize-Giving', 'The Spelling Prize', from *Selected Poems*, ETT Imprint; Seamus Heaney: 'Scaffolding', 'Mid-Term Break', 'The Play-Way', from *Death of A Naturalist*, Faber and Faber Ltd; Russell Hoban: 'Typo', from *The Pedalling Man and Other Poems*, Grosset and Dunlop Inc., by permission of David Higham Associates; Philip Hodgins: 'Snap shot', 'Place Kick', 'Drop Kick', from *A Kick of the Footy*, HarperCollins Publishers Australia, 'The Meaning', 'The Snake in the Department Store', 'Giorgio de Chirico', from *Things Happen*, HarperCollins Publishers Australia; Ted Hughes: 'The Horses', 'Leaves', from *New Selected Poems 1957-1994*, Faber and Faber Ltd; Paul B. Janeczko: 'Stars', copyright 1991, Paul B. Janeczko, reprinted by permission of the author; Andrew Lansdown: 'Sometimes in the Dark', 'Against the Wall', from *The Grasshopper Heart*, reprinted by permission of the author; John Laue: 'Around the High School', first published in *English Journal*, USA, reprinted by permission of the author; George MacBeth: 'Fourteen Ways of Touching the Peter', from *The Night of Stones*,

Macmillan Publishers Ltd; **Lorraine Magi-Williams:** 'Mimi Dancers', reprinted by permission of the author; **Brenton Mander:** 'Snake', from *A Book to Perform Poems By* edited by Rory Harris and Peter McFarlane, Australian Association for the Teaching of English; **Gerda Mayer:** 'Ballard', © Gerda Mayer, 'Ballard' was first published in *New Angles Book 2*, published by Oxford University Press, 1987, by permission of the author; **Roger McGough:** 'The Examination', from *Waving at Rains*, Jonathan Cape, 1982; Pete Morgan: 'The Television Poem', by permission of the author and David Higham Associates Ltd; **Pablo Neruda:** 'They Come for the Islands (1493)', translated by W. S. Merwin, from *Selected Poems* edited by Nathaniel Tarn, published by Jonathan Cape Ltd, reprinted by permission of the Estate of the author, translator and Jonathan Cape; **Oodgeroo of the tribe Noonuccal (formerly Kath Walker):** 'We Are Going', 'The Curlew Cried', 'Colour Bar', from *My People 3rd Edition*, 1990, published by Jacaranda Press; **Wilfred Owen:** 'Arms and the Boy', from *The Collected Poems of Wilfred Owen* edited by C. Day Lewis, by permission of the Estate of the author and Chatto & Windus; **Geoff Page:** 'Pine Tree', from *Paperback Poets 5: Two Poets*, 1971, University of Queensland Press; **Peter Porter:** 'A Consumer's Report', from Peter Porter's *Collected Poems* (1983), by permission of Oxford University Press, Oxford; **William Random:** 'Not Enough Dough!, Tough!', from *Young Writer's Tales*, Macmillan Publishers Ltd; **Jennifer Rankin:** 'Forever the Snake', from *Collected Poems*, 1990, University of Queensland Press; **Vernon Scannell:** 'Love', 'The Pop Star's Song', from *Love Shouts and Whispers*, reprinted by permission of the author and Hutchinson as publisher; **Ian Shaw:** 'Simply Being Jim', reprinted by permission of the author; Peter Skrzynecki: 'Immigrants at Central Station, 1951', from *Immigrant Chronicle*, 1975, University of Queensland Press; **Wallace Stevens:** 'Thirteen Ways of Looking at a Blackbird', from *The Collected Poems of Wallace Stevens*, Faber and Faber Ltd; **Gwen Strauss:** 'The Waiting Wolf', from *Trail of Stones*, Julia MacRae; **Jennifer Strauss:** 'Migrant Woman on a Melbourne Tram', from *Winter Driving*, Sister Publications, 1981, reprinted by permission of the author; **May Swenson:** 'Analysis of Baseball', 'Seven Natural Songs', 'Over the Field', 'Living Tenderly', from *More Poems to Solve*, Charles Scibiner's Sons; **Colin Thiele:** 'Car Salesman', from *Selected Verse*, Rigby, reprinted by permission of the author; **Judith Wright:** 'The Surfer', from *Collected Poems*, ETT Imprint; **Nikolai Zabolotsky:** 'The Face of the Horse', from *Scrolls*, translated from Russian by Daniel Weissbort, Jonathan Cape; **Robert Zend:** 'When', 'Pencil', from *Zero to One*, Sono Nis Press, Victoria, Canada 1973.

Paintings:

Georges Braque: *The Bird*, © Georges Braque, reproduced by permission of VI$COPY Ltd, Sydney 1997; **Giorgio de Chirico:** *The Great Game (Italian Square)*, © Giorgio de Chirico, 1971, reproduced by permission of VI$COPY Ltd, Sydney 1997; **Pieter de Hoogh:** *Woman Peeling Apples*, Wallace Collection, London; **Russell Drysdale:** *The Cricketers*, 1948, Private Collection; **L.S. Lowry:** *Man Lying on a Wall*, City Art Gallery & Museum, Salford.

Every effort has been made to trace the original source of copyright material contained in this book. The publisher would be pleased to hear from copyright holders to rectify any errors or omissions.